HIP ASIAN
COMFORT FOOD

A Tasting of Jacksonville's Blue Bamboo Restaurant

To: Lisha,
Best wishes for
Happy Hip Asian Dishes!
- DC

DENNIS CHAN

Published by Blue Bamboo Publishing Co.
3820 Southside Boulevard
Jacksonville, Florida 32216

904.646.1478 orders
www.bluebamboojacksonville.com

Printed and designed by Raintree Graphics, Inc.
Printed and bound in the United States of America.

Text edited by Kim Benton
Photography by Linda Blakely
Photo selection by Gladys Ova

ISBN 978-0-615-25869-0

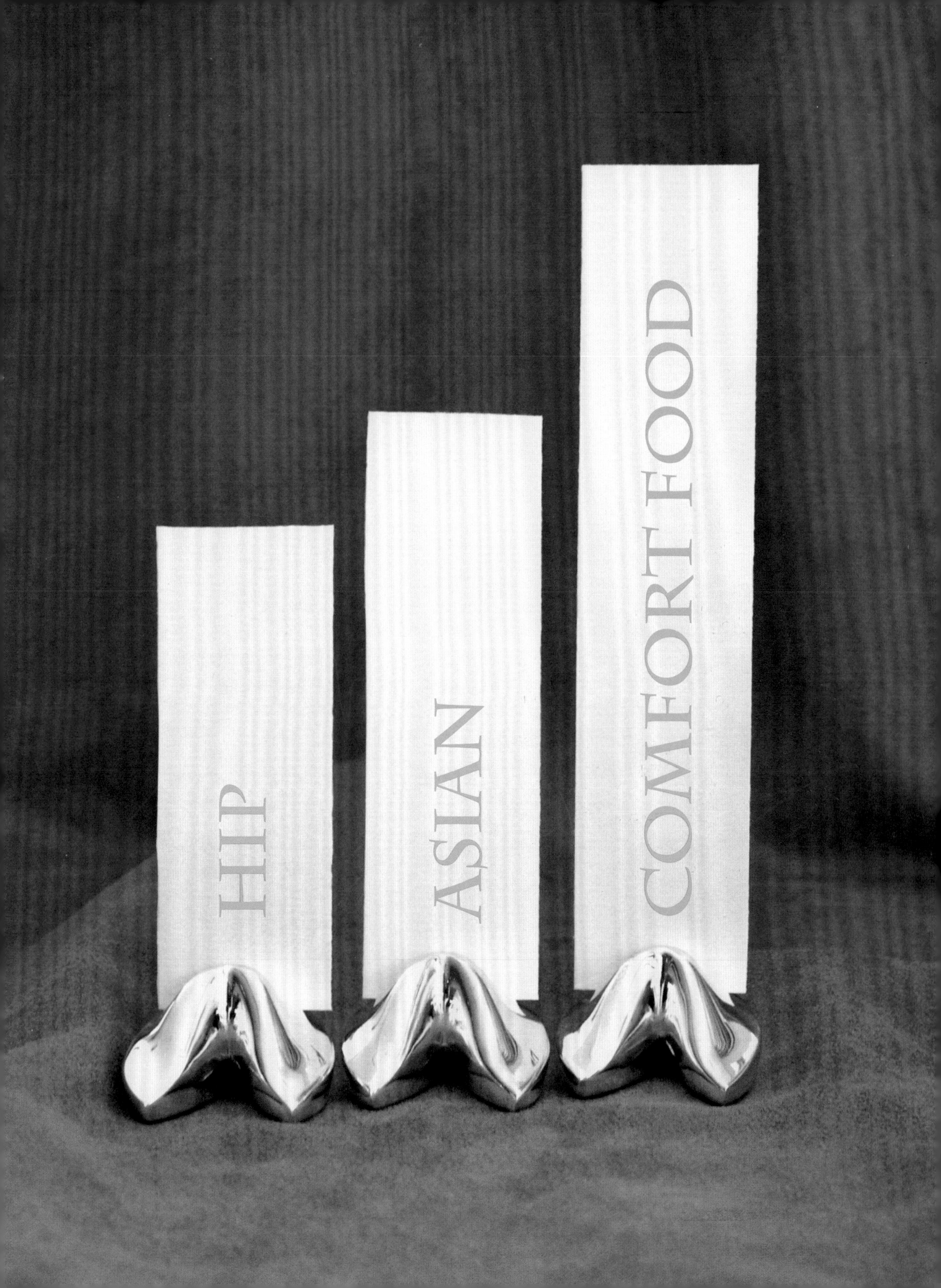
HIP
ASIAN
COMFORT FOOD

FOREWORD

I've known Dennis Chan for ten years. In that decade, I've watched him grow and evolve from a green, culinary school extern at Blue Ginger to the confident, executive chef/owner of Blue Bamboo, his restaurant in Jacksonville, Florida.

Dennis was our first intern at Blue Ginger, witnessing not only how to break down Thai lime leaf for an aioli, but also the bumps along the road of opening a new restaurant. He worked practically every station at Blue Ginger at some point, helping out with whatever was necessary — always a smile on his face, enthusiasm never flagging. That's how I knew he would one day own his own restaurant. You not only need culinary skills, but you need drive and, most importantly, the love of it.

Dennis and I cook the same kind of cuisine: East-West — meaning, ingredients and techniques from both the East and the West, combined harmoniously. At Blue Bamboo, you can expect to start the meal with spareribs and end with crème brulee — and it will all make perfect sense — and of course, taste delicious!

"Hip Asian Comfort Food," Dennis's first cookbook, offers some of the best kinds of comfort food Asia has to offer. Sometimes, there's nothing better than slurping a big bowl of noodles or digging into a platter of fried rice — it just makes you feel taken care of. This is also a great cookbook if you're craving a more modern take on the standards — with recipes like Red Curry Shrimp and Grits and Chile Noodle Salad Forks — Dennis's take on East-West food is all about keeping what's great about Asian flavors and ingredients and giving them new life with exciting presentations and preparations.

I hope you enjoy "Hip Asian Comfort Food" and turn to it often when you're craving something different than your usual standards.

Peace & Good Eating,

Ming Tsai
Chef/Owner, Blue Ginger, Wellesley, MA
Host/Executive Producer, "Simply Ming"

CONTENTS

ACKNOWLEDGMENTS

I would like to first thank my parents, Ming and Phyllis, for all the opportunities you have given me. Thanks for making it possible for me to do exactly what I love and accomplish my childhood dream.

Thanks to my cousin May, who was my first boss at our family restaurant, Little Dragon. Look at what you have started.

Thanks to Ming Tsai, for taking the chance on a culinary student and hiring me as his first intern at Blue Ginger, and for telling me, "Whatever you name your restaurant, it's gotta have the word BLUE in it." Hey, it worked.

Thanks to my Uncles and Aunts for all their love and never-ending support.

I would like to thank the staff of Blue Bamboo. The restaurant is lucky to have your time and positive energy. Your hard work and care for our guests continues to WOW me!

Thanks to Linda Blakely for your amazing photography talent and friendship.

To Kim Benton, who kept us on schedule and provided printing expertise way beyond my imagination.

And finally, thanks to the guests of Blue Bamboo. You have been very supportive, and helped our business grow tremendously over the past few years. Word of mouth is the best advertising, and I appreciate your loyalty. Thanks for letting us serve you. It has been a real privilege, and I am grateful for your confidence in us!

THE STORY OF BLUE BAMBOO

My love of food started when I watched my grandfather cook in his classic Chinese restaurant, Eng's Golden Dragon, in the 70's. I was too small to remember the techniques, but there was a small red stool that I stood on to see what he was cooking in the pot. Little did I know that this was where my kitchen instincts would be set into motion. Since then, my family has owned twelve successful restaurants in Jacksonville, Florida.

Food is woven tightly in our family culture. If we are not thinking about the food we are eating, then we are thinking about food that we have eaten, or thinking about the food we are going to eat. I knew that I had a family legacy to continue by opening Blue Bamboo, coupled with my desire to create contemporary food, with a nod toward traditional flavors.

My father did whatever he could to discourage me from the restaurant business. As an academic, he wanted me to study, not hang out in the family business. However, I couldn't help but grow to love the restaurants. My first job was working at my cousin's restaurant, Little Dragon. There was something social about the time that I was there, a real camaraderie. We all worked together to focus on the customer. Today, I still enjoy the company of the same people I used to work with at Little Dragon.

While attending University of Florida, I came home on the weekends to work at my aunt's restaurant, Mandarin Dragon. Here, I learned that regular customers could establish lifelong relationships. To this day, I still see those same customers who ate with my family back then.

The time at UF was a time of discovery. Although I had grown up with these Asian roots, I had no connection to them and an opportunity arose to study abroad in China. I would love to tell you that the food in China was incredible, but it wasn't. As a chunky kid, I loved to eat and that time in China made me lose 50 pounds. Everything was either white or brown. The rice, which was white, had rocks in it, and the meat was brown. The vegetable of the season was cauliflower. If we skipped rice for a meal, then we ate steamed bread. Yuck! It was not until I got to Hong Kong that I saw green vegetables again, and vibrant colored food.

I knew that if I were to open my own restaurant and follow my family legacy, I had better learn my way around a professional kitchen. I attended the Culinary Institute of America, in Hyde Park, New York. Many people go to that school to learn how to cook, but I learned how to eat!

My goal with this cookbook is to provide you with simple recipes filled with bold Asian flavors. Your time is precious, and with your busy lifestyle, I couldn't think of a better way to make our Asian cuisine a part of your every day life.

Since the day Blue Bamboo opened, I never wanted it to be a stuffy restaurant, with stuffy service. I love that people feel comfortable here, and our food shows it. This cookbook contains nothing fussy, just Hip Asian Comfort Food from my table to yours. Enjoy!

STREET EATS

In Asia, people eat by going to street vendors, ordering a different course from each stall until they are full. We have adopted that style of dining here at Blue Bamboo. Here is a selection of "Street Eats" that will serve as appetizers, or when you pair a few of them together, make a great meal.

BASIC GRILLED SALMON SALAD WITH MANGO SALSA

Salmon is a healthy fish that is a great source of the Omega 3 fatty acids that keep your heart tickin'. The Mango Salsa is simple, quick to make, and goes perfectly with the salmon.

For perfect grill marks, place the oiled salmon on the grill, let it sear, and rotate 90 degrees. Then, let it sear again. Flip and cook the other side until done.

Serves 4

4-8 oz salmon filets, for grilling
1 tbsp unflavored oil*
8 oz spring lettuce mix
2 tbsp balsamic vinegar
2 tbsp olive oil
Salt and pepper to taste

Mango Salsa

1 mango, diced
½ red pepper, diced
1 tsp cilantro, chopped
1 tbsp fresh lime juice
Salt and pepper to taste

Combine Salsa ingredients. Set aside. Rub salmon with oil. Season with salt and pepper, then grill until done. Toss spring mix with olive oil, vinegar, salt, and pepper. Center greens on plate. Top with Grilled Salmon filet and Salsa.

*Note: Unflavored oil can be any cooking oil that does not have strong flavors such as canola oil, grape seed oil or extra light tasting oils.

PANKO-CHEESE CRUSTED TOMATOES

You can thank my Mom for this recipe. Being a Southern woman, she loves her fried green tomatoes. One day, shortly after we opened, we were playing around in our kitchen, and fried up some tomatoes in Japanese bread crumbs. Mom loved them, and we served this recipe to the Junior League ladies for a special event. Their approval is what landed these tomatoes on our menu, where they have remained ever since.

Serves 4

2 cups Japanese Panko bread crumbs*
1 cup buttermilk
8 Roma tomatoes, sliced thick
1 cup rice flour
Salt and pepper to taste
Unflavored oil, for frying
Parmesan cheese, for garnish

Tomato-Cheese Salsa

2 Roma tomatoes, diced
1 tbsp Parmesan cheese
2 basil leaves, chopped
Salt and pepper to taste

Combine Salsa ingredients. Set aside.

Cover tomatoes in rice flour. Dip in buttermilk. Roll in Panko bread crumbs. Fry in 350°F oil until golden brown.

Top with Parmesan cheese and Tomato-Cheese Salsa.

*Note: This standard breading technique is the best way to fry anything. I always say that my favorite flavor is *fried*. The trick to breading is keeping one hand wet and one hand dry. That way, you don't end up with "Monster Hands," having gobs of bread crumbs and sticky flour on them. This recipe also works great for shrimp, oysters, and chicken.

BLUE BAMBOO
FLAX SEED CRACKERS

This is one of many recipes that make us famous. We serve flax seed crackers to every guest who comes through our doors. Flax seeds are good for you, and they provide a rich plant source of Omega 3 oils and fiber to keep your heart healthy. My Mom and our longtime family friend, Cindy, make these crackers at the restaurant. The rest of us love grabbing them hot out of the oven, as we walk by the bakeshop in our kitchen.

Yields 35 crackers

1 cup flax seeds
3 cups all-purpose flour
1 tsp baking powder
½ tsp salt
1 oz butter, softened
1 cup milk

Using a table-top mixer, combine dry ingredients and butter. Use a paddle attachment to mix until ingredients resemble coarse meal. Add milk to mixture until it forms a soft dough ball. Wrap in plastic wrap and refrigerate for 30 minutes.

Turn dough onto lightly floured counter and roll into $\frac{1}{16}$th inch thickness. Cut dough into 2-inch strips or triangles. Place on cookie sheet. Bake at 325°F for 20 minutes or until crisp and golden.

Allow crackers to cool and store in an airtight container.

COCONUT MILK CHICKEN SOUP

This is our most popular soup. It is based on a classic Thai soup called Tom Kha Gai. Our version keeps people coming back with its fragrant, tart, and coco-nutty flavor. Our mildly spicy soup features the flavor of galangal, which creates a heavenly taste. Coconut Milk Chicken Soup opens your taste buds, and it's a great beginning to any meal. A larger portion of the soup is good enough to make ahead for a quick lunch.

Serves 4

2 lbs chicken, cooked and shredded
1 cup coconut milk, thin
1 cup coconut milk, thick
1 cup chicken stock
2 tbsp fish sauce
2 tbsp lime juice
2 slices ginger
8 slices galangal*
2 cloves peeled garlic
1 stalk lemongrass
4 kaffir lime leaves
2 fresh chiles, seeds removed
Salt and pepper to taste

Cilantro Oil

½ bunch cilantro
1 cup unflavored oil

In a blender, combine cilantro and oil and puree. Set aside.

Combine thin coconut milk, chicken stock, galangal, garlic, lemongrass, lime leaves, ginger, and chiles. Bring to a boil. Reduce heat and simmer for 15 minutes. Add chicken, thick coconut milk, fish sauce, lime juice, salt, and pepper. Return to a boil. Remove from heat, strain, and serve garnished with Cilantro Oil and shredded chicken.

*Note: Galangal is a root that looks like ginger's older, darker, tougher cousin. It is often used in Southeast Asian cooking for its spicy, gingery flavor.

CHOP SUEY SALAD

I wanted to take a classic dish, like Chinese Chop Suey, and prepare a version of it with fresh vegetables and those yummy crunchy noodles. This easy recipe is great for entertaining. At catered parties, we serve the salad in paper takeout boxes with chopsticks.

Serves 4

¼ head iceberg lettuce, shredded
¼ cup carrots, shredded
1 cup napa cabbage, shredded
¼ cup celery, shredded
¼ red pepper, slivered
¼ red onion, sliced
Salt and pepper to taste

2 each spring roll wrappers, sliced and fried

Sesame Ginger Dressing

2 tbsp sesame oil
1 tsp ginger, minced
1 tsp soy sauce
½ cup oil
1 tsp scallion, chopped
1 tbsp rice wine vinegar

Combine dressing ingredients and blend. Fry spring roll wrappers at 350°F until golden brown and season.

Toss ingredients in dressing. Season to taste with salt and pepper.

How We Roll...

I learned how to make sushi from one of my mentors, Ming Tsai, who learned from a sushi master in Japan. When we opened *Blue Bamboo*, we had no intention of serving sushi. Our guests kept asking for it, and I called up my friend, Teddy, who is a sushi expert.
Together, we "rolled out" a sushi menu, and today, sushi is a big part of our business!

SUSHI

Makes 3 rolls, 24 pieces

1 cup sushi rice
2 cups water
½ cup seasoned rice vinegar
3 sheets seaweed
Sesame seeds, to sprinkle
Stuffing, of your choice
Sesame seeds for garnish
Wasabi and pickled ginger for garnish

Bring to boil rice with 2 cups water and cover. Turn down the heat and simmer for 20 minutes. Turn off heat. Let sit covered for 15 minutes. Turn out rice to a bowl. Season with rice vinegar and let cool.

Flatten out a baseball-sized amount of seasoned rice onto the seaweed over a sushi mat. Sprinkle with sesame seeds and turn upside down on mat.

Place a strip of ingredients in center of the seaweed. Roll, tucking in the ingredients back into itself, lifting mat as you push forward.

Re-shape roll, cut into pieces, and arrange on the plate.

Boiled Pierogi Potstickers

Pierogies are a staple in Eastern European cooking and are the Polish version of filled dumplings. If time is of the essence, make the dumplings by using store-bought wonton skins. The key to a good Pierogi is a well-seasoned stuffing.

Serves 2

Pasta

1½ cups all-purpose flour
2 eggs
½ cup water
½ tsp salt

Filling

1 lb potatoes, boiled and mashed
2 medium onions, finely chopped
1 tsp salt
½ tsp black pepper

Sauce

1 cup heavy cream
1 cup Parmesan cheese
Fresh sage, 5 sprigs

Combine the flour, eggs, water and ½ tsp salt. Knead mixture. Let rest for 30 minutes.

Sauté onions until golden and mix with 1 tsp salt and ½ tsp pepper, then mix onions into potatoes.

Cut the dough into two equally sized pieces and roll each one into a cylinder. Cut each cylinder into 1-inch pieces, then roll into a very thin 2-inch circle (or use wonton skins).

Put 1 tbsp of filling in the center of each circle. Fold the dough in half and seal the edges with egg. Pinch the corners together.

Boil the potstickers in salted water for seven minutes or until they float to the surface.

Warm cream, ½ cup cheese, and sage. Serve potstickers with sauce and sprinkle with Parmesan cheese.

FRIED DRAGON WHISKERS

We opened *Blue Bamboo* in a space which housed a Chinese restaurant called The Dragon, and they had a successful business for 15 years. We wanted to honor their success by naming an appetizer after the former business. We created Dragon Whiskers, which are delicious zucchini straws garnished with cheese to say, "Hey, thanks for the space and the ancestry."

Serves 4

8 oz zucchini, julienned
Rice flour, as needed for breading
Buttermilk for soaking
Salt and pepper to taste
Ranch dressing as dip
Parmesan cheese as needed
Unflavored oil, for frying

Preheat oil to 350°F

Soak zucchini in buttermilk to wet. Dredge in rice flour, while keeping each strand separate. Place coated zucchini in a fry basket, and shake off the excess coating.

Deep fry until lightly golden and crispy. Drain on paper towels.

Season with salt and pepper. Garnish with grated Parmesan cheese. Serve with your favorite ranch dressing.

*Note: Julienne cut in chef talk is a long, thinly sliced cut.

ROAST DUCK SPRING ROLLS

Occassionally, we are asked to do multi-course duck tastings. Here's how we start off every duck tasting.

Serves 4

½ lb roast duck, pulled off bone
4 oz re-hydrated mung bean noodles*
1 cup shredded cabbage
½ cup shredded carrots
¼ cup sliced green onion
Salt and pepper to taste

20 frozen spring roll skins, defrosted
Egg, for sealing
Unflavored oil, for frying

Soak mung bean noodles in salted hot water until soft. Drain and rinse under cold water.

Prepare all ingredients. Mix and season filling.
Roll ingredients in spring roll skins.

Fry in 350°F oil until golden-brown, and delicious. Drain on paper towels, and serve with Apricot Duck Sauce.

Apricot Duck Sauce

½ cup apricot preserves
1 cup applesauce
½ cup red pepper, sliced
Salt and pepper to taste
Honey, to taste

Heat small saucepan. Add ingredients and bring to boil. Cool and let stand for 1 hour. Add salt and pepper to taste.

*Note: Mung bean noodles, also called bean thread noodles, are thin noodles made from Mung beans. To soften them, soak for about 10 minutes in warm water. They can be found in the Asian aisle at your local grocery store.

PEANUT-LIME CHICKEN SALAD

This is my version of a steakhouse salad using a honey-lime vinaigrette and peanuts. It is our biggest seller at lunch and is always a hit for catered parties. You can also add mandarin oranges for a nice, added tartness, or use the dressing on noodles for a delicious pasta salad.

Serves 6

1 pound mixed greens
Carrots, sliced into strips
Salt and pepper to taste
4 grilled chicken breasts, cubed
Peanuts, chopped

Dressing
½ cup sweet chile sauce
¼ cup soy sauce
2 oz pickled ginger*
½ cup peanut butter
1 tbsp garlic, chopped
1 tbsp lime juice
½ qt peanut oil
2 tbsp rice wine vinegar
2 tbsp honey

Process dressing ingredients in a blender. Reserve to dress salad.

Toss greens and carrots with dressing.

Add chicken and salt and pepper.

Plate and garnish with peanuts.

Note: Pickled ginger or *gari* is a classic Japanese accompaniment. It is available at your local supermarket in the Asian aisle.

VIETNAMESE SUMMER ROLLS

These delicious and healthy rolls are unfried and full of flavor. In culinary school, I craved them so badly, that I made my own version and created this perfect formulation. Add a Peanut Sauce or Nuoc Cham Sauce to delight your senses.

Makes 1 roll

2 slices roast pork (optional)
1 broiled shrimp (optional)
2 oz rice stick noodles, re-hydrated
1 piece rice paper, re-hydrated
½ oz carrots, cut into matchsticks
Fresh Thai basil leaves
Fresh garlic chives, whole
Fried shallots, dried
Black and white sesame seeds, for garnish
Salt and pepper to taste

Re-hydrate rice noodles in warm water for 20 minutes. Drain and set aside.
Prepare all ingredients, and cut all vegetables to size.

Soak rice paper for 3 seconds in a shallow pan of warm water. Place sheets on a clean towel.

Roll ingredients in shell. Garnish with sesame seeds.

Vietnamese Peanut-Hoisin Dipping Sauce

1 tsp unflavored oil
2 garlic cloves, minced
2 tbsp chile paste
4 tbsp chunky peanut butter
4 tbsp hoisin sauce
4 tbsp water
Salt and pepper to taste

Heat small saucepan. Add oil and garlic. Fry until golden, then add hoisin sauce. Add other ingredients and bring to boil. Cool and let stand for 1 hour for flavors to meld. Season with salt and pepper to taste.

Nuoc Cham Sauce

2 crushed garlic cloves
2 tbsp sugar
2 tbsp fresh lemon juice
1 fresh chile, sliced
¼ cup rice wine vinegar
¼ cup fish sauce
Shredded carrots and daikon for
    garnish

Bring all ingredients to a boil. Let cool. Garnish with shredded carrots and daikon radish.

PULLED PORK WONTON EMPANADAS

When I travel to major cities that have a large Chinese population, I always seek out a good dim sum restaurant. Here's my version of *Hip* Asian dim sum, which takes Asian flavors and infuses them with a little Latino accent.

Serves 6

1 lb pork shoulder, cut into large chunks
2 cups mirepoix*
1 tbsp fermented dried black beans
1 tbsp tomato paste
½ cup soy sauce
1 cup hoisin sauce
6 dried shitake mushrooms
5 cloves garlic
1 tbsp cumin
1 package potsticker skins
1 egg

Garlic Chive Mojo

2 cloves garlic
1 jalapeno pepper, seeded and minced
2 tsp toasted cumin seeds
½ tsp salt
1 small bunch garlic chives
½ cup unflavored oil
2 tbsp rice wine vinegar
Salt and pepper to taste

Brown pork pieces. Remove from pan. Add mirepoix, garlic, black beans, and tomato paste to pan. Cook vegetables until soft. Add hoisin sauce, and deglaze with soy sauce and water to cover ingredients in pot. Add shitakes and pork. Simmer slowly for 3-4 hours. Refrigerate overnight.

Pull pork into small pieces. Place 1 tbsp of pulled pork into the center of the wonton skins and seal with egg. Fry at 350°F until golden brown.

Braising liquid can be reduced to garnish. Serve with Garlic Chive Mojo.

Finely chop garlic, pepper, and garlic chives. Transfer to a blender. Add salt and cumin. Drizzle in oil and vinegar. Salt and pepper to taste.

*Note: Mirepoix is the combination of vegetables used as a flavoring for a soup or sauce. The traditional ratio for mirepoix is 2 parts onion, one part carrot, and one part celery. Use whatever tastes good to you, or whatever the market has on sale that day. Leeks, scallions, and shallots may be substituted for onions. Parsnips may be substituted for the carrots. Be creative. If you stick to the ratio, it will taste good.

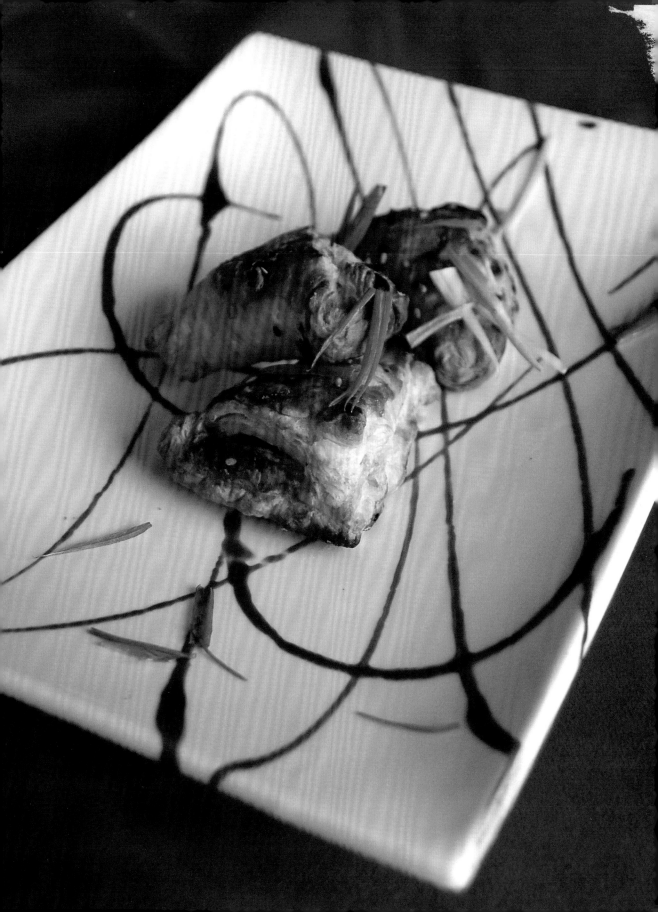

CHILE NOODLE SALAD FORKS

We make these simple salad forks for catered events. Every year, we participate in Caring Chefs, an event to benefit a local children's organization. This salad keeps people coming back every year to our booth. We like to present it already twirled on forks so that it is easy to eat. It also makes for a beautiful presentation on a tray for cocktail parties.

Serves 4 as a small course, or 20 for a cocktail party

1 lb string pasta, cooked al dente
1½ cups sweet chile sauce
1 cup fresh cilantro, chopped
2 tbsp garlic
1 tbsp ginger
½ cup soy sauce
¼ cup scallions, chopped
1 red pepper, chopped
2 carrots, shredded
Salt and pepper to taste

Cook pasta until al dente. Shock the pasta in ice water to stop cooking and drain.

Mix remaining ingredients with pasta. Season with salt and pepper. Allow pasta to combine with flavorings.

Using a spoon or spoodle, twirl pasta on forks. Lay out on tray for guests. This salad can also be served in rice bowls with chopsticks for a quick lunch.

RICE FLOUR ONION STRAWS

I am often asked about our batters and breadings. These Onion Straws are a perfect example of our basic fry coating. It also works well with thinly sliced vegetables and meats. These straws also make a great garnish for salads. Eat them soon after they are fried.

Serves 4

2 red onions, sliced thin
2 cups buttermilk
1 tbsp ginger, minced
1 lb rice flour
1 tsp kosher salt
1 tsp freshly ground black pepper

Unflavored oil, for frying

Season the rice flour with salt and pepper. Mix well. Mix ginger into buttermilk. Slice onions, and dip into buttermilk mixture, then into flour. Coat well.

Shake all excess flour off, and fry at 350°F until golden. Drain on paper towels and season with salt and pepper.

Serve with your favorite ranch dipping sauce.

Knife and Fork Nuoc Mam Caesar Salad

Classically, Caesar salads are made tableside. The dressing is made right in front of you, and the salad is served immediately. The ingredients are simple. Our version uses a Vietnamese fish sauce to give the dressing an extra richness. In Southeast Asia, people use fish sauce as their seasoning instead of salt or soy sauce. We like to keep the lettuce leaves whole so that you have to eat it with a knife and fork.

Serves 4

2 hearts of romaine, separated and washed
1 pasteurized egg yolk
1 garlic clove
2 tbsp Vietnamese fish sauce
½ cup olive oil
¼ cup freshly grated Parmesan cheese
Salt and pepper to taste

Croutons

¼ loaf day-old crusty bread
2 tbsp olive oil
1 tbsp Parmesan cheese
Salt and pepper to taste

Cut bread into large cubes. Toss in olive oil and Parmesan cheese until coated. Season with salt and pepper. Bake at 350°F until golden. Let cool.

In a bowl, smash garlic clove with egg yolk. Add fish sauce. Slowly drizzle in olive oil and Parmesan cheese. Season with salt and pepper.

Toss in romaine lettuce and serve with croutons.

Chinese BBQ Ribs

Every time these go out into our dining room, my mouth waters. My parents used to sell 4,000 pounds of ribs every week at their little drive-thru restaurant on the Northside of Jacksonville. I have always loved these Chinese BBQ Ribs. The sauce is hoisin based, but we glaze it with some honey just as they are coming off the grill. They are red, just like they have been for decades, and the Chinese believe that red is a good luck color.

Serves 4

Sauce

2 cups hoisin sauce
½ cup soy sauce
½ cup ketchup
1 tbsp ginger, minced
1 tbsp garlic, minced
1 tbsp red food coloring
½ cup honey
Honey for glazing
2 slabs spareribs

Mix all sauce ingredients together. Spread all over ribs. Bake covered in foil for 2 hours at 325°F.

Fire up grill, and reheat ribs on grill top. Baste with honey at last minute, cut, and serve.

TUNA CEVICHE

Ceviches are sexy. Our trendy Asian version adds the flavors of sesame and ginger to the traditional lime flavoring of this dish.

Serves 4

1½ lbs tuna loin, diced
½ red pepper, diced
½ red onion, diced
1 tbsp ginger, grated
2 tbsp sesame oil
1 clove garlic, minced
¾ cup lemon juice
¼ cup lime juice
2 Roma tomatoes, diced
1 cup corn kernels, cooked and cooled
½ tsp cumin, ground
Salt and pepper to taste

Cut tuna into dice-sized pieces. Mix with lemon juice, lime juice, ginger, sesame oil, and garlic. Place in the refrigerator for 2 hours.

Dice the remaining ingredients, toss with the tuna mixture. Serve with Plantains and Garlic Mojo.

Garlic Mojo

2 cloves garlic
1 jalapeno pepper, seeded and minced
2 tsp toasted cumin seeds
½ tsp salt
1 small bunch garlic chives
½ cup neutral oil
2 tbsp rice wine vinegar or lime juice
Salt and pepper to taste

Finely chop garlic, pepper, and garlic chives. Transfer to blender, puree, add salt and cumin. Drizzle in oil and vinegar. Add salt and pepper to taste.

Fried Plantains (Tostones)

Unripe Plantains
Oil for frying
Salt to taste

Cut plantains into 1½ inch pieces. Fry in 350°F oil until browned. Remove from oil and smash to about ¼ inch thickness. Fry again until golden brown. Lift plantains out of the oil and season with salt.

BASIL CHICKEN LETTUCE WRAPS

This is the most authentic Thai item on our menu, and the wraps have a hint of spice with a slightly sweet kick. The fragrant Thai basil is what takes the experience up to another level of delightfulness.

Serves 4

1 tbsp garlic, minced
1 tbsp unflavored oil
2 chicken breasts, cubed for stir frying
1 tsp ginger, minced
2 tsp dried chilies, crushed
2 tbsp sugar
2 tbsp fresh lime juice
2 tbsp fish sauce
1 red onion, sliced
2 green onions, cut into 2 inch pieces
½ cup peanuts
4 sprigs Thai basil

Iceberg or bibb lettuce, for wrapping

Prepare all ingredients. Heat wok to medium heat and sauté garlic in oil until fragrant. Add chicken and ginger, and sauté until almost done. Add chilies, sugar, lime juice, red onion, and fish sauce. Stir until heated. Add green onions, peanuts, and basil.

Plate and serve with lettuce.

SOUTHERN KATSU GRIT CAKES

Here's something to do with your leftover grits from the Red Curry Shrimp and Grits recipe (see page 79). These are a great brunch or side item. We even make miniature versions of the cakes for cocktail parties. Katsu is the Japanese method of breading and frying. What a perfect match…Southern and Japanese.

Serves 4

1½ cups cooked grits, cooled
½ cup sautéed onions
Salt and pepper to taste

Breading

2 cups Japanese bread crumbs
1 cup buttermilk
1 cup all-purpose flour
Salt and pepper to taste

Unflavored oil, for frying

Sauté onions until translucent. Set aside and let cool.
Form cold grits and sautéed onions into patties.

Bread patties by using the following standard breading procedure below:
1. Coat with flour
2. Dip in buttermilk
3. Coat with bread crumbs

Fry at 350°F until golden brown. Drain on paper towels.

These cakes are delicious with Mango Salsa (see page 12), or with a classic tonkatsu* sauce.

*Note: In Japan, tonkatsu is a quick meal of a breaded meat or poultry cutlet on rice. The traditional sauce for this meal is part ketchup, part worchestershire sauce, and part BBQ sauce. It's a delicious, slightly tangy sauce that is a great accompaniment to fried foods.

SWEET POTATO POTSTICKERS

These potstickers are a fun appetizer for cocktail parties. We stuff them with a sweet potato mixture. Your guests will be pleasantly surprised at the delightful combination of seasoned sweet potatoes and onions.

Here's a tip: you can fry them and serve with a dipping sauce, or boil and serve with a cream sauce as a side dish.

Serves 4

2 lbs sweet potato, steamed
½ lb butter, softened
1 tsp nutmeg
1 small onion, sliced and sautéed
1 package of wonton wrappers (round or square)
1 egg, beaten
Unflavored oil, for frying

Mash sweet potatoes, butter, nutmeg, onions, salt and pepper together. Fold 1 tbsp of mixture into each wrapper, sealing with egg and making a half-moon shape.

Fry at 350°F until golden brown. Drain on paper towels.

CURRY PEANUT CHICKEN SATAY

Satay's are easy to eat, and great for cocktail parties and for cookouts. I first tasted satay at one of my aunt's family gatherings. She is from Southeast Asia, and the flavor combination was incredibly light and fresh tasting to the palate.

Serves 4

1½ lbs chicken breast or beef, sliced thin
20 bamboo skewers, soaked
1 can coconut milk
2 tbsp fish sauce
Curry powder, for dusting
Salt and pepper to taste

Cut chicken breast into ½ inch slices. Marinate in coconut milk, fish sauce, and curry powder for 3 hours or overnight. Soak skewers for a half hour prior to use. Thread chicken onto skewers. Season skewers and sauté or grill until done.

Cucumber Relish

1 English cucumber, sliced thin
2 shallots, sliced
2 tbsp cilantro, chopped
½ cup rice wine vinegar
3 tsp sugar
¼ tsp salt
Chopped peanuts for garnish

Combine all ingredients. Set aside.

Curried Peanut Sauce

1 can coconut milk
1 tbsp green or Massaman curry paste
¾ cup peanut butter
¼ cup brown sugar
2 tbsp fish sauce

Combine all ingredients. Bring to a boil. Cook and stir until sauce is well blended. Store in refrigerator until ready to use.

WONTON SAMOSAS

One of our regular guests said "The way to an Indian's heart Is just to say the word, *Samosa*." We only make them a few times throughout the year and are delighted to taste-test them when we can. We make 2 chutneys to compliment these Samosas.

Serves 6

2 lbs ground lamb or chicken (optional)
2 small onions, diced
2 tbsp garlic, chopped
2 tbsp curry powder
1 tbsp garam masala*
2 lbs steamed potatoes, mashed
½ lb frozen peas
1½ cups tomatoes, diced
1½ cups coconut milk
Unflavored oil for sautéing
Wonton wrappers
Egg, beaten, for sealing
Unflavored oil for frying
Salt and pepper to taste

Sauté onion, garlic, and lamb for 10 minutes. Add spices. Add tomato, coconut milk, and reduce to sauce consistency.

Add potatoes and peas. Season to taste.

Cool in fridge. Fill and form wonton wrappers into triangles. Seal with egg.

Fry in 350°F oil. Drain on paper towels.

*Note: Garam masala is an Indian spice mixture that is slightly spicy and contains dried chile, black pepper, cumin, corriander, cardamom, cinnamon, and cloves. There are many variations of this mixture. If you visit Indian markets, you can find the mixture whole. You'll need to toast and grind it yourself, but you get a better flavor that way.

Mango Chutney

3 mangoes, peeled and grated
1 lb fresh ginger, peeled and grated
3 garlic cloves
½ cups cider vinegar
2 cups sugar
½ tsp turmeric
3 dried chiles, whole
Salt and pepper to taste

Put all ingredients into saucepan and bring to a boil. Lower heat and simmer for 30 minutes, until thick. Yields 3 cups.

Tamarind Chutney

¼ cup tamarind*, seeded
1¼ cups boiling water
1 tsp cumin
1½ tsp ginger
½ tsp cayenne
¼ cup dates
3 tbsp peanuts
1 tbsp coconut, dried unsweetened
1 tsp salt
1 tbsp cilantro, chopped

Place all ingredients in blender. Blend until smooth. Cover and let flavors meld for 3 hours.

*Note: Tamarind is a tart, pulpy fruit used in Southeast Asian cooking. You can find it in your local Asian market.

CHICKEN STICKS WITH BRAZILIAN-STYLE SALSA

Chicken Sticks have been a staple on our menu since day one. The coating on the chicken is crispy, and the chicken stays nice and juicy when fried. My culinary school classmate gave me the recipe for a salsa that is amazing and full of flavor. We have found that salsa pairs well with our chicken sticks.

Serves 4

2 lbs chicken breast meat, cut into 2-inch pieces

Breading

2 cups Japanese bread crumbs
1 cup buttermilk
1 cup all-purpose flour
Salt and pepper to taste
Unflavored oil, for frying
Bamboo skewers

Brazilian Salsa

1 cup Roma tomatoes,
　peeled and seeded
½ cup red onions, diced
1 bell pepper, diced
½ bunch parsley, chopped
¼ cup water
⅓ cup red wine vinegar
1 tsp whole grain mustard
½ cup olive oil
Salt and pepper to taste

Combine all ingredients for salsa. Chop in food processor. Adjust salt and acidity to taste. Set aside.

Bread the chicken pieces by following standard breading procedure (flour, buttermilk, and then bread crumbs).

Fry at 350°F until golden brown. Drain on paper towels. Season with salt and pepper.

Skewer each chicken piece and serve on top of salsa.

CRISPY-SPICY OYSTERS

These oysters will be the best that you have ever tasted. Only buy fresh oysters in the "R" months (Fall and Winter). The oysters we purchase are from the northern part of the Gulf of Mexico. The chile flakes in this recipe are usually used for kimchi, the spicy fermented cabbage that is used to accompany most Korean meals.

Serves 4

3 cups Japanese Panko bread crumbs
2 cups buttermilk
20 oysters, shucked
2 cups rice flour
¼ cup chile flakes
Salt and pepper to taste

Unflavored oil, for frying

Cover oysters in rice flour.
Dip in buttermilk.
Roll in Panko bread crumbs, seasoned with chile flakes.

Fry in 350°F oil until golden-brown and delicious.

Season with salt and pepper and present in cleaned oyster shells or Chinese soup spoons. Serve with your choice of dipping sauce.

PALATABLE POTABLES

Our beverage program is a huge part of our success at Blue Bamboo. We have a great wine list, and a great mixed beverage list. We have just as much fun coming up with recipes for our bar as we do for our kitchen. It took us a long time to get our full beverage license, but once in place, we wasted no time in creating our unique beverage menu. It's part of what makes us Hip.

SAKE WHITE SANGRIA

Many of our cocktails use sake as a base. Not only is sake very mixable, but also compliments many other flavors. Sangria is one of the new favorite beverages on the dining scene. Our *Hip* version is made with white wine and sake.

Makes 6 Sangrias

1 bottle of white wine
½ cup sugar
3 oranges, sliced
½ cup of orange juice
1 lemon, sliced
1 lime, sliced
1 apple, diced
½ liter of ginger ale
1 cup sake

Pour wine in a pitcher and squeeze the juice wedges from the orange, lemon and lime into pitcher. Add sugar, orange juice, and apple. Chill overnight.

Stir. Add ginger ale and sake just before serving. Serve with citrus wedges and a cherry.

GIRL SCOUT COCKTAIL

When I was growing up in Jacksonville, Florida, our family would see the Girl Scouts come every year to fill our order of thin mint cookies. The combination of mint and chocolate in this drink reminds me of those delicious Girl Scout cookies.

Makes 1 Cocktail

1 oz dark crème de cocoa liqueur
1 oz green crème de menthe liqueur
Splash of cream

In a glass, pour in all ingredients.
Stir. Add ice.

Bubble Tea

In Asia, it's *Hip* to hang out in bubble tea houses. The cool attention-grabber in teahouses is their shaking machines. The barista makes your tea in a cocktail shaker, and then places it in a machine that shakes the beverage. 'Bubble tea' gets its name from the bubbles that form on milk tea after it has been shaken. Often times, bubble teas are served with giant tapioca pearls. Once you've had one, and gotten over the strange huge pearl texture, you'll want more.

Makes 4 Bubble Teas

Tapioca Pearls

1 cup extra large pearls
2 quarts water
½ cup brown sugar

Boil 2 quarts water in a large pot. Add 1 cup tapioca pearls to boiling water. Boil for 25 minutes, covered. Turn off heat. Let pearls sit in water for ½ hour. Rinse. Sprinkle with ½ cup brown sugar and set aside until ready to serve.

Tea

6 cups water
½ cup Thai red tea leaves
2 tbsp black tea leaves
1 cup sugar
1 cup evaporated milk

Bring water and sugar to a boil. Add the tea leaves and remove from heat. Steep for 5 minutes. Strain through a filter and add evaporated milk. Store in refrigerator until ready to use.

Pour tea in shaker with ice. Shake until well chilled. Spoon tapioca pearls into glass. Pour shaken tea into glass. Sip bubble tea and tapioca pearls through large straw.

Lemongrass Martini

Lemongrass is an herb that gives you the fragrance of lemon without the acidity. In a local farmers' market, there was an herb grower who had lemongrass plants. I bought two of them, and they are now planted at the restaurant, ready for us to use any time.

Makes 1 Martini

Lemongrass-infused vodka
Splash of lemongrass syrup
Crushed ice
Lemongrass stalk for garnish
Pink peppercorns for garnish

Chop lemongrass stalks and place into infusion jar. Cover with vodka and let sit for 3 days.

Add ice, 4 oz infused vodka, and 2 oz lemongrass syrup. Shake. Strain. Garnish with a lemongrass stalk and pink peppercorns.

Lemongrass Infused Syrup

2 cups water
1 cup sugar
6 stalks of lemongrass (white part only)

Thinly slice lemongrass. Bring all ingredients to a boil. Let cool, store in refrigerator overnight.

GREEN TEA MARTINI

If you are in the mood for something exotic, but not fruity, this is the perfect mixed drink for you. It contains a hint of peach schnapps that adds a smooth tartness to this martini.

Makes 1 Martini

3 lemon slices, muddled*
1½ oz green tea concentrate
½ oz peach schnapps
1 oz vodka
Chilled martini glass

To make green tea concentrate, take 1 oz green tea powder and dilute into 5 oz hot water. Cool and reserve for use.

In a mixing glass, muddle lemon slices. Pour in all ingredients. Add ice and shake. Strain the mixture into a chilled martini glass.

*Note: Muddling is bar speak for smashing.

GINGER MILKSHAKE

Ginger is refreshing, and it has proven medicinal effects. It is said to be a native of Asia and will warm your soul with its healing properties. This milkshake pairs well with our Soy-Glazed Burger. The best comfort food...a warm, fresh burger and a milkshake.

Makes 1 Milkshake

2 scoops vanilla ice cream
1 cup whole milk
1 cup ice
2 oz ginger syrup
Candied ginger* for garnish

Place ingredients in a blender and blend until smooth.

Garnish with candied ginger.

Ginger Syrup

2 cups water
1 cup of sugar
1 palm-sized piece of ginger

Thinly slice ginger. Bring all ingredients to a boil. Cool in refrigerator until needed.

*Note Candied ginger is available in your grocer's baking aisle.

CUCUMBER-LIME SAKTAIL

One of our servers created this drink, which is refreshing any time of year. This is our up-town Asian version of a Mojito. A perfect Saktail or shaken martini has chards of ice floating on the top. You'll know it when you see it.

Makes 1 Saktail

1 piece cucumber
1 piece lime
1 oz simple syrup*
2 oz vodka or sake
Chilled martini glass, lime

Smash, or as professional bartenders say, muddle cucumber and lime together in a mixing glass. Add ice, syrup, and sake or vodka. Shake, strain the mixture into a chilled martini glass, and garnish with a lime.

*Note: A simple syrup is an equal amount of sugar and water by volume boiled until it is uniform.

Try this for dessert or drink it with our rice flour onion straws on page 35. Either way, you'll feel like you are in the ultimate Asian comfort food diner. We make this with an Italian-style ginger soda.

One of the ice creams in our secret stash at *Blue Bamboo* is ube, or taro ice cream. Taro is the root of the elephant ear plant, and Asians use it in savory and sweet dishes. We usually keep an ice cream made from it on hand for snacking.

Makes 1 Float

8 oz soda water
1½ oz ginger syrup
3 oz scoop ube ice cream* (taro ice cream)

In a tall, iced glass, pour in ginger syrup and soda water. Garnish with
ube scoop. Stir before drinking.

Ginger Syrup

2 cups water
1 cup sugar
1 palm-sized piece ginger

Thinly slice ginger. Bring all ingredients to a boil. Cool and refrigerate until ready to use.

*Note: Ube ice cream can be found at your local Asian market.

A friend of mine in Orlando taught me this recipe. One evening, she made me one of these fruit punches and told me, "It's the best you'll ever know." When I tasted the drink, I totally agreed. Now, when we make it for our guests, no one stops at just one.

Makes 1 Fruit Punch

2 oz pineapple juice
2 oz orange juice
1 oz cranberry juice
2 oz lemon-lime soda
½ oz grenadine
Ice

Combine all ingredients in glass.
Shake. Serve.

VIETNAMESE COFFEE MARTINI

Forget any espresso martini that you have ever tasted…ours is the best! Vietnamese coffee has the flavor of chicory in it, and it makes a fabulous martini.

Makes 1 Martini

1 oz shot chicory coffee espresso
1 oz vanilla vodka
1 oz coffee liqueur
Splash of cream
Thin chocolate ganache* or syrup for garnish

In a mixing glass, pour in all ingredients. Add ice and shake. Strain into a chilled martini glass, pre-garnished with chocolate syrup or ganache.

*Note: Ganache is a chocolate and milk mixture. It can be very thin, like a chocolate sauce, or very thick, like a fudge.

THAI ICED RED MILK TEA

Thai restaurants all over the country make their own version of Iced Red Milk Tea. Even as a classically trained chef, I had to try many recipes before I got it just right.

Makes 4 Red Milk Teas

6 cups water
1 cup Thai red tea leaves
1 cup sugar
1 cup evaporated milk

Bring water and sugar to a boil. Add tea leaves and remove from heat. Steep for 5 minutes. The tea will turn dark orange. Strain through a filter and refrigerate until ready to use.

Add ice, and tea to ¾ full. Add 3 tablespoons of evaporated milk per glass.

Shake or stir.

THAI-GARITA

We first mixed this drink for Cinco de Mayo. It became such a hit that we have kept it on the menu ever since. It's a great, refreshing drink to make for pool parties. Multiply the recipe by 10 to make a pitcher. Ice it down just before serving.

Makes 1 Thai-Garita

½ oz lemon juice
1 oz lime juice
½ oz triple sec
1½ oz tequila
1 oz sake

In a mixing glass, pour in all ingredients.

Add ice and shake.

Strain into a chilled martini glass, garnished with a lime wedge.

MANGO RUM LASSI

Lassi is a refreshing yogurt drink from India. It cools your pallet and serves as a great pairing for "heat" that is usually found in traditional Indian dishes. Yogurt makes this concoction healthy because it contains bone friendly calcium and is low in fat.

Makes 1 Rum Lassi

3 oz mango juice
1 tbsp simple syrup*
1 tbsp plain yogurt
5 oz whole milk
2 oz dark rum
Ground cardamom and mint for garnish

Fill a highball glass with ice. Pour in ingredients and shake. Pour into chilled glass and garnish with ground cardamom and mint (optional).

*Note: A simple syrup is an equal amount of sugar and water by volume boiled until it is uniform.

Iced Chicory Coffee

You can find Vietnamese espresso presses that will fit over a standard glass at any Asian market. They are perfect for making the slow-dripped espresso needed for this drink. The Chicory Coffee by itself is strong, but when blended with condensed milk, it becomes perfection in a glass.

Makes 1 Coffee

2 tbsp chicory coffee
⅔ cup boiling water
⅓ cup sweetened condensed milk

Place ground coffee beans in press.
Screw on top screen and place over condensed milk in glass.

Pour water over press and let drip.

Stir and add ice.

Ginger Mojito

Latin cooking and Asian cooking are similar in ingredients, but not in technique. I've created this version of a Cuban favorite that is very refreshing.

Makes 1 Mojito

Juice of 1 lime
1 oz ginger syrup
2 mint sprigs
Ice
2 oz light rum or sake
Cold sparkling water

Smash 1 mint sprig in bottom of glass. Add ice, lime juice, 2 oz of rum or sake, and ginger syrup. Fill with sparkling water and shake. Garnish with a fresh mint sprig.

Ginger Syrup

2 cups water
1 cup sugar
1 palm-sized piece ginger

Thinly slice ginger. Bring all ingredients to a boil.

Let cool, store in refrigerator overnight.

POSMOPOLITAN

Some people call this the ultimate girly-drink. The Posmopolitan is our most popular martini and it's made with pomegranate. Infused with sweetness and citrus, this timeless drink will certainly delight the senses.

Makes 1 Martini

1 wedge lime, muddled*
1 wedge orange, muddled*
1½ oz sake or vodka
½ oz triple sec
½ oz cranberry juice
½ oz pomegranate juice

Muddle fruit in cocktail shaker. Add sake or vodka, triple sec, pomegranate and cranberry juices. Shake with ice. Strain into chilled martini glass.

Garnish with a lime wedge.

*Note: Muddling is bar speak for smashing.

One of our regular guests requested that we make Chai Tea for a catered event. It was a cold winter afternoon and the Chai Tea was perfect for warming up guests who relaxed by the fireplace. What makes chai so delicious is the addition of vanilla and spices to strong black milk tea.

Makes 4 Chai Teas

6 cups whole milk
2 cinnamon sticks
1 vanilla bean or 2 tbsp vanilla extract
1 cup sugar
2 tbsp black tea

Bring milk and sugar to a boil. Add cinnamon and tea and remove from heat.

Steep for 10 minutes. Strain contents through a filter and into a coffee mug.

If you would like to make an iced version, refrigerate, and pour over ice.
Top with whipped cream.

THE BEST WAY TO PAIR WINES WITH YOUR FOOD.

Wine pairing takes a little experimentation, but when you have your first perfect pairing of food and wine, you are always on the quest to find the next perfect pairing.

Body. When we talk about body, we mean how wine coats your mouth. Think of milk… whole, 2%, and skim. The way milk coats your mouth is how a full, medium, and light bodied wine coats your mouth, respectively. Fuller bodied wines will pair best with fatty, full flavored foods. Lighter bodied wines will pair best with lighter, more delicate foods. Grapes, from lighter to fuller body are: Pinot Grigio, Sauvignon Blanc, Chardonnay, Pinot Noir, Merlot, Cabernet, Syrah and Zinfandel.

Flavors. When we talk about a flavor of a wine, we mean what you taste when the wine hits your tongue. It can have the flavor of cherries, vanilla, oak, mineral, peaches, apples, or berries.

Nose. When we talk about the nose of the wine, that means – how does it smell? Sometimes, you smell flowers or herbs. Other times it is grass and maybe even tobacco.

WINE GUIDE

Wines that pair well with our Hip Asian Cuisine.

California Pinot Noir: These wines were made popular by a movie a couple of years ago. They generally have a lot of cherry flavor, and a lot of bright herbs. This wine is an excellent compliment to our Pan Fried Noodles.

Italian Barbera: This is a light and very flavorful wine. It's high in acid, which makes it pair well with foods that contain nuts, like our Rama Thai Stir Fry.

Viognier: This wine is very floral, with a lot of apricot and peach flavor. It has slight acid, which is good for mellowing out some of the richer buttery sauces. Try it with our Basil Lettuce Wraps.

Alsatian Riesling: These wines have a lot of acid. They have enough body to be a good pairing for our Tuna dishes.

French Sancerre from the Loire Valley: Light-bodied with a floral nose, this wine will pair well with our dishes that contain basil, such as our Summer Rolls.

Beaujolais: A light bodied red wine that has a lot of fruit. This wine pairs well with cheese dishes. Our Panko Tomatoes are a great match for this wine.

Sparkling wine from Champagne, France: This wine is made from a classic blend of 3 grapes, which makes it pair well with a wide range of seafood dishes such as our Green Curry Shrimp and Salmon.

French and Italian Rosés: Generally, rosés are light, bright, and full of aroma. They pair well with food, but are great just for sipping on the front patio at Blue Bamboo!

Zinfandel: These wines are full of heavy fruit, like cherries, plums, and raspberry. Zinfandels tend to have a peppery edge to them, which make these full-bodied wines perfect for our Sichuan Peppercorn-Crusted Steak.

Burgundian Chardonnay: This wine has a good amount of mineral, but also has enough acid to cut through anything fried. It's a good match for our Panko Oysters.

Pinot Grigio: A very uncomplicated wine, Pinot Grigio, or Pinot Gris, pairs well with light salads. They are usually high acid, but make for great summertime sipping.

New Zealand Sauvignon Blanc: These wines are known for their explosive grapefruit flavor and a lot of acid. They drink well with our Crabcakes.

French Vouvray: These wines tend to be light and fruity. Try them with our Satay.

Santa Barbara Pinot Noirs: With a nice crisp red fruit, and aromatic nose, these wines pair well with our Pulled Pork Empanadas.

Prosecco: Proseccos are Italian sparkling wines. They are missing the minerality of French sparking wines, so they pair really well with tomato and cheese dishes, like our Panko-Crusted Tomatoes.

Argentinan Malbecs: Have dark, smoky flavors that pair well with our steaks. Like our Sichuan Peppercorn Filet. It's still a little heavy for the steak itself, but when served with fries, it's a match.

Chardonnay: From France, you can expect a lot of mineral. These pair well with our Nuoc Mam Caesar Salad. From the USA, there is usually a lot of oak and vanilla and butter. Try them with something fried, like our Grit Cakes.

Bordeaux: Is an area that produces red wine made from Cabernet, Merlot, and Cabernet Franc grapes. Try this one with Shaking Beef.

California Syrahs: Have a lot of fruit and pair well with peppery foods. A great match would be our Soy Glazed Burger.

White Rhone Blends: Such as a Marsanne-Rousanne blend are a great match for curry. Our Curried Wonton Samosas are great with these wines.

Chateauneuf Du Pape: Is mainly a blend of Syrah and Grenache. It has a slightly spicy flavor, and a slightly meaty taste. It pairs well with the Korean Braised Short Ribs.

Burgundy Pinot Noir: Duck and Pinot Noir are a classic pairing. Try our Hip Asian pairing with Vietnamese Curry Noodles with Duck.

Italian Chianti or Dolcettos: Pairs well with our Curry-Lime Pasta. Italian sauces, also very high in acids, pair well with these wines. That makes our pastas a natural for these wines.

Banyuls Port: Port wines are perfect matches for any chocolate dessert. Try them with our brownie.

Royal Tokaji: Is an amazing Hungarian wine that has incredible honey notes. It has a hint of citrus, and is a natural selection for our Mandarin Orange Cake.

Sauternes: These sweet, but high-in-acid wines classically pair with foie gras. Try them with Crème Brulee, also rich and creamy.

Brachetto d' Acqui: This has fun bubbles. It is just slightly sweet and is delicious with our Red Tres Litchis Cake.

P L A T E S

What defines us and helps make our entrees hip at Blue Bamboo is our plating. We love presenting food in ways our customers would never expect. Our plates are served in a casually sophisticated setting and always with inviting and comfortable Asian style.

CHICKEN POT PIE

When this plate is served to a table, the overwhelming response is, "That's not pot pie." Once the guest takes the very first bite, they can't say another word. The crust is usually the best part of a pot pie, and we've made it the focal point of the dish. To add texture, we coat our chicken with Panko bread crumbs then fry until golden brown and delicious.

Serves 4

2 lbs chicken breast meat, cut into 2-inch pieces
2 cups Japanese Panko bread crumbs
1 cup buttermilk
1 cup all-purpose flour
Salt and pepper to taste
Unflavored oil, for frying

Bread chicken pieces by following standard breading procedure. (Flour, buttermilk, and then bread crumbs.)

Fry at 350°F until golden brown. Drain on paper towels.

Filling

½ cup broccoli, diced
½ cup carrots, diced
½ cup zucchini, diced
1-10 oz can cream of celery soup
¼ cup sherry
2 cups cream
Parmesan cheese to taste
Salt and pepper to taste
1 sheet puff pastry, thawed

Combine cream of celery soup, cream, sherry, and vegetables in saucepan. Bring to a boil. Cook until vegetables are tender. Season with salt, pepper, and cheese. Serve over fried chicken pieces. Bake puff pastry according to manufacturer's directions. Place on top of dish.

Green Curry Shrimp and Salmon

Our Green Curry Shrimp and Salmon is the heartiest recipe on our menu. Rarely will people finish this plate, but they will always take the rest home. The curry paste adds interesting flavor that can also be used for soups and vegetables.

Serves 4

4-8 oz pieces of salmon
1 tbsp green curry paste
2 tbsp lime juice
2 tbsp fish sauce
12 oz coconut milk
2 cups mixed vegetables
1 tsp ginger, minced
½ tsp garlic, minced
1 lb shrimp, peeled and de-veined
Salt and pepper to taste
Unflavored oil, for sautéing

Make sauce by sautéing green curry paste and adding liquids. Let the ingredients come to a boil. Simmer for 10 minutes. Set aside.

Season the salmon with salt and pepper. Coat with oil and grill or sauté.

While salmon is grilling, sauté shrimp with ginger and garlic in a separate pan until almost done. Add vegetables. Top with sauce and let simmer until vegetables are tender.

Plate the curry and salmon on top of Jasmine Rice. (see page 130)

Spicy Hoisin Chicken Stir Fry

We wanted to put a contemporary spin on this comfort food while keeping all the flavor of the classic Sichuan chicken. Our version leaves out the greasy sauce from the original version. If you're not feeling like "chicken tonight," try substituting any kind of meat. The beauty of a stir fry is the ability to use whatever ingredients you like.

Serves 2

½ lb chicken breast, cut into strips
2 cups total: onions, peppers, and carrots, cut into
   uniform sized pieces
1 tsp ginger, chopped
1 tsp garlic, chopped
1 tsp scallion, chopped
1 tbsp oil
3 tbsp hoisin sauce
1 tbsp cooking wine
1 tbsp sambal or sriracha*
1 tbsp sesame oil
½ cup broth
Salt and pepper to taste

Heat wok. Add oil. Swirl to coat pan. Sauté ginger, garlic, and scallion until fragrant. Add chicken and cook until almost done. Add vegetables and broth. Bring to a boil. Cook until vegetables are tender. Season with hoisin sauce, sambal, sesame oil, salt, and pepper. Serve over steamed rice.

*Note: Sambal is a coarse chile paste made in Vietnam. Sriracha is a more finely pureéd version of the same sauce.

GENERAL'S CHILE-SOY CHICKEN

Before we opened *Blue Bamboo*, one of my favorite takeout items was General's Chicken. The combination of soy and chiles makes this traditional dish tart, spicy, savory, and sweet. We wanted to do a version for our menu, so we used the same flavors but breaded the chicken in Panko bread crumbs. The Panko adds a nice crispy and crunchy texture to this recipe.

Serves 4

2 lbs chicken breast, 2 oz pieces pounded thin
6 oz soy sauce
4 oz sweet chile sauce
3 oz each water and vinegar
1 oz sriracha* chile paste
Sugar, to taste
4 oz red pepper, cut into matchsticks
4 oz onion, cut into matchsticks
2 cups buttermilk, as needed
1 cup all-purpose flour, as needed
1 cup Japanese Panko bread crumbs

Serve with steamed Jasmine Rice (see page 130).

Bread chicken using standard breading procedure:
Set up 3 pans or plates with flour, buttermilk, and bread crumbs. Dip chicken in flour, then buttermilk. Roll chicken in Panko. Fry at 350°F until golden, and chicken is cooked throughout.

Heat sauté pan. Add water and vinegar, soy, sweet chile sauce, sriracha, sugar, and vegetables to pan. Sauté until vegetables are done. Pour sauce over chicken and serve with Jasmine Rice.

*Note: Sambal is a coarse chile paste made in Vietnam. Sriracha is a more finely puréed version of the same sauce.

RED CURRY SHRIMP AND GRITS

Our new signature dish at *Blue Bamboo* is our Red Curry Shrimp and Grits. For Mother's day brunch, we feature the classic recipe from the Carolina coasts. We added our own *Hip* Asian touch by making our grits with red curry, a true marriage of Asian comfort food and Southern cooking. Try making the grits ahead of time, and serving the Red Curry Shrimp with the grit cakes on page 41. It's what you see in the picture, and the crispy texture of the cakes takes the dish to another level.

Serves 2

1 cup grits
3 cups chicken stock
1 tbsp red curry paste
1 tbsp unflavored oil
12 oz coconut milk
2 tbsp lime juice
1 tbsp fish sauce
1 onion, sliced
1 red pepper, sliced
1 lb shrimp, peeled and de-veined
Salt and pepper to taste
Sriracha to taste

Heat red curry paste in pan with oil in pan. Add coconut milk, fish sauce, and lime juice. Bring to a boil and simmer for 5 minutes. Reserve half of mixture for shrimp topping. Bring remaining sauce to a boil with 2 cups of stock. Whisk in grits. Gradually add in remaining stock, as needed. Cover pan. Grits will splatter when cooking. Cook to grit manufacturer's time recommendation.

In a separate pan, sauté shrimp, onions, and red peppers until done. Add reserved sauce, and pour over bowl of cooked grits.

COCONUT-LEMONGRASS CRAB CAKES

These crab cakes have been on our menu since the day we opened. Lemongrass is a woody herb that contains all the flavor of lemon, without any of the acid. Use only the lower ⅓ of each stalk. The top portion of the plant does nothing for flavor. To get the most flavor out of each stalk, trim the end, crush with the side of a cleaver or knife, finely slice, and then mince. You can find lemongrass fresh or dried at any Asian market.

Makes 8, 4 oz cakes, Serves 4

½ lb lump crab meat
1 lb backfin crab meat
½ red pepper, minced
1 tbsp garlic chives, chopped
1 egg
¼ cup mayonnaise
2 tbsp dijon mustard
1 tsp crab boil seasoning
½ tsp salt
½ tsp black pepper
1 cup panko bread crumbs
2 tbsp unflavored oil, for searing

Sauce

½ cup coconut cream
2 tbsp lemongrass, minced
Salt and pepper to taste

In a large bowl, mix all ingredients for crab cakes, being careful not to break lumps. Let sit in refrigerator for 1 hour.

Heat coconut cream with lemongrass. Remove from heat and let steep. Season with salt and pepper. Strain just before serving.

Shape crab cakes into 4 oz patties, 1-inch thick. Heat skillet. Add oil. Sear both sides of crab cakes. (about 3 minutes per side) Serve with coconut-lemongrass sauce and dressed greens.

SICHUAN EGGPLANT

You can use Chinese eggplants, the longer, paler purple varieties, or the Italian deeper, rounder varieties for this dish. The key is frying them first. The last time I made this recipe it was for someone who didn't think they liked eggplant until they tried my version. It's a little sweet, a little spicy, and sure to delight your senses.

Serves 2

1 lb eggplants, cut into chunks
2 tbsp honey
1 tbsp soy sauce
1 tsp chile flakes, dried
¼ cup orange juice
1 tbsp ginger
1 tbsp garlic
1 tbsp scallion
Salt and pepper to taste
1 tbsp oil, for sautéing, and more for frying

Cut eggplant into chunks. Fry at 350°F until golden. Drain.

Heat wok. Add oil, chile flakes, ginger, garlic, and scallions. Sauté until fragrant. Add juice, honey, and soy. When sauce starts to bubble, add eggplant and coat evenly. Serve with hot steamed rice.

SICHUAN PEPPERCORN FILET
WITH ROSEMARY HERBED FRIES

The first time that a guest sits down at a table and sees filet on our menu, they are surprised. Our restaurant is sometimes described as "ostensibly Asian." Call it what you want, but filets are my favorite cut of steak because they are tender without a lot of marbling. This simple recipe is one of the best ways to prepare this steak using mildly hot Sichuan peppercorns that adds a crunchy texture to the steak's surface. You can find the peppercorns in any Asian market.

Serves 1

Sichuan peppercorns, cracked
Black peppercorns, cracked
Salt
1-8-10 oz beef filet
1 potato, cut into ½ inch fries
½ tbsp rosemary, fresh-picked and chopped
Salt and pepper to taste

Generously season filet with salt, pepper, and Sichuan peppercorns. Place on open flame grill or heated iron skillet. Flip once, and grill to desired temperature.

Rinse starch off potatoes. Fry fries in 275°F oil for about 5 minutes. Drain on paper towels. Fry again in 350°F oil until golden brown. Drain again. Season with salt, pepper, and rosemary while fries are still slightly wet. Serve fries alongside steak.

Ginger Smoked Turkey with Cracklin' Corn Bread

Last Thanksgiving, one of our customers asked me to prepare a turkey for him. I brined 3 turkeys and set up a smoker behind the restaurant. The brining took 2 days in our walk-in cooler. If you have an ice-chest, and plenty of ice, you can brine at home. Preparing it this way will give you the juiciest turkey you will ever taste.

Serves 6

Brine

3 bunches sage, fresh or dried
3 tbsp dried oregano
1 hand-sized piece of ginger, minced
2 cups sugar
2 cups kosher salt
2½ gallons water, or enough to submerge the
    turkey
Turkey bag or clean food-grade garbage bag
1 10-12 pound turkey

Dissolve brine ingredients in water. Place in bag with turkey. Seal and place in bucket or cooler in fridge. Keep temperature under 41°F until ready to roast or smoke.

Roast or smoke according to package directions. Stop cooking when a thermometer inserted into thigh reaches 155°F.

Cracklin' Cornbread

2 cups cornmeal
1 tsp baking soda
3 tsp sugar
¼ tsp salt
2 cups buttermilk
½ cup cracklins, broken into small pieces
2 tbsp butter or shortening

Preheat oven to 350°F.

Sift dry ingredients into a mixing bowl and combine.

Add buttermilk and stir. Fold in cracklins and butter or shortening. Place in a greased 8 inch baking dish and bake for 30 minutes.

Cut into 2-inch squares and serve warm.

STEAMED WHOLE FLORIDA SNAPPER

We are often asked for whole steamed fish. In fact, it has become so popular that we brought in a dedicated wok range just for steaming. We take classic steamed fish one step further and add an Orange-Cilantro Splash. The citrus and cilantro combination is also great on chicken.

Serves 2

2 lbs snapper, cleaned and scaled
Ginger, sliced
Scallion
Salt and pepper to taste

Prepare the snapper by cutting slits in the flesh on both sides. This will help the fish stay flat when you steam it. Place a piece of ginger in each incision. Season the fish with salt and pepper. Steam fish until done. It will take approximately 15 minutes. Sprinkle scallions on fish. Heat orange-cilantro vinaigrette until very hot and splash onto fish. Skin will sizzle.

Serve with steamed rice.

Orange-Cilantro Splash

½ bunch cilantro
1 cup olive oil
Juice of 1 orange
2 tbsp soy sauce
Salt and pepper to taste

Clean and dry the cilantro. Put leaves into blender. Add salt, soy, and juice.

Drizzle oil into moving blender.

Vinaigrette will keep for 1 week in the refrigerator.

BLUEBERRY BBQ PORK TENDERLOIN

Healthy blueberries lend a unique flavor to this incredibly tender pork tenderloin. Around Jacksonville, there are a few 'pick your own' blueberry farms. Whenever you can connect with your food at its source, somehow it always tastes better!

Serves 4

Sauce

4 cups blueberries
½ cup chopped celery
½ cup chopped onion
½ cup chopped green pepper
3 garlic cloves, minced
½ carrot, minced
½ cup honey
1 tbsp molasses
⅔ cup vinegar
1 tbsp paprika
½ tsp cinnamon
Pinch ground nutmeg
Pinch dry mustard
½ tsp celery seed
½ tsp ginger, minced
Cayenne, salt and pepper to taste

Sauté celery, onions, green pepper, garlic, and carrots in saucepan. Add honey, molasses, vinegar, and spices.

Add berries. Simmer over medium heat, stirring occasionally, until thickened. Puree entire mixture in blender or use a stick blender in saucepan.

Refrigerate until needed, sauce will keep in refrigerator for 1 week.

Pork Tenderloins

2-12 oz pork tenderloins
1½ cups blueberry BBQ sauce
Salt and pepper to taste

Season pork tenderloins with salt and pepper. Grill or sear all sides of tenderloins. Baste pork with sauce and place in 350°F oven until internal temperature of meat reaches 145°F.

SEARED SHERRY-YAKI CHICKEN

The combination of sherry, orange, and ginger in this recipe makes your tongue say WOW!
What makes this dish wonderful is that it is quick and easy to make. You may already have the
basic ingredients on hand. We entered it in a local sherry distributor's recipe contest and won!

Serves 4

2 lbs chicken breast, cut into 2 oz pieces, pounded thin
½ cup all-purpose flour
2 tbsp oil
Salt and pepper to taste
¼ cup sherry
2 tbsp soy sauce
½ tbsp ginger, minced
1 cup heavy cream
2 tbsp orange juice
¼ cup grated Parmesan cheese

Dredge pounded chicken pieces in flour. Heat oil in pan. Season chicken with salt and pepper.
Sear on both sides until almost done. Add sherry, soy sauce, ginger, orange juice, and cream.
When sauce bubbles, sprinkle Parmesan cheese and remove from heat. Serve with steamed rice
and vegetables.

PANKO FRIED CHICKEN

Chicken and creamed peas is a Jacksonville tradition. Many local restaurants provide this meal combination. We play with the old favorite of fried chicken by using Panko bread crumbs. Panko is popular with Japanese meals and makes whatever you coat it with very crispy and crunchy.

Serves 4

4-8 oz chicken breasts
2 cups buttermilk
1½ cups Japanese Panko bread crumbs
1 cup all-purpose flour
Unflavored oil, for frying
Salt and pepper to taste

Dredge chicken breasts in flour. Dip in buttermilk. Coat in Panko bread crumbs. Fry in 350°F oil until golden brown and cooked throughout.

Season with salt and pepper.

Creamed Peas

1 lb peas, frozen or fresh, shelled
2 tbsp all-purpose flour
2 tbsp butter
½ cup sugar
1 quart heavy cream
Salt and pepper to taste

Combine butter, sugar, and flour in saucepan. Whisk or stir in cream. Heat until thickened. Add peas and bring to a boil. Simmer for 5 minutes, and remove from heat.

Serve chicken and creamed peas with biscuits.

BLUE BAMBOO BASIC STIR FRY

Our guests are always intrigued by stir frying. In our cooking classes, the feedback that we receive is always strongest when we incorporate a stir fry technique in the class. Here is a recipe for an easy stir fry. You can change any of the recipe components to suit your needs. The technique is great for making a quick dinner. The most difficult part in stir frying is the preparation of all your ingredients. In French, it is called mise en place. I just call it "get your act together." In all stir fries, ginger, garlic, and scallions are the basic seasonings.

Serves 4

½ lb beef, chicken, pork, or shrimp, cut into strips
2 cups vegetables, cut into uniform size pieces and blanched
1 tbsp ginger, chopped
1 tbsp garlic, chopped
1 tbsp scallion, chopped
1 tbsp oil
3 tbsp oyster sauce
½ cup broth
Salt and pepper to taste

Heat wok or pan. Add oil. Swirl to coat pan. Sauté ginger, garlic, and scallion until fragrant. Add beef, chicken, pork or shrimp. Cook until almost done. Add vegetables and broth. Bring to a boil. Season with oyster sauce, salt and pepper.

Serve over steamed rice.

Kung Pao Tofu

Here is one of our favorite vegetarian dishes that is even popular with meat eaters.
The hoisin sauce in this dish clings to the tofu, and gives it a fabulous flavor. Sriracha chile paste is a chile-garlic blend, made in Vietnam. Some people tell me they use this sauce like ketchup in their homes. Substitute any protein for the tofu and create your own kung pao!

Serves 4

16 oz firm tofu, cut into triangles
1 bell pepper, sliced
1 onion, sliced
1 tbsp unflavored oil
3 tbsp hoisin sauce
1 tbsp sriracha sauce
1 tsp sesame oil
2 tbsp cooking wine
2 tbsp peanuts, crushed
Salt and pepper to taste
Unflavored oil, for frying tofu

Fry tofu at 350°F until golden. Remove and drain on paper towels.

Heat oil in pan. Add vegetables and sauté until warmed through. Add tofu, and stir in liquids. Season with salt and pepper. Dish is ready when sauce starts to bubble.

Serve with steamed Jasmine Rice.
(see page 130)

Soy Grilled Lamb Rack

Last year, we had to plant a rosemary garden behind the restaurant because this dish is so popular. So we went to our local garden shop and bought live plants. Our little herb garden variety has grown since we first planted our rosemary bushes. It now includes cilantro and lemongrass. Fresh cilantro makes a great mango salsa that is delicious with traditional rack of lamb. The tart and spicy mango salsa cuts the heartiness of the lamb nicely.

Serves 2

1 lb rack of lamb
Salt and pepper to taste
2 sprigs fresh rosemary, chopped
½ cup fresh parsley, chopped
3 cloves garlic, minced
2 oz olive oil
2 tbsp soy sauce

Marinate lamb rack with ingredients. Sear in hot pan or over open flame. Roast until internal temperature reaches a minimum of 140°F. Serve with Spicy Mango Salsa and a drizzle of Cumin-Carrot Oil.

Spicy Mango Salsa

1 mango, diced
1 jalapeno, diced
Juice of 1 lime
1 tbsp chopped cilantro
½ red pepper, diced
Salt and pepper to taste

Combine all ingredients.
Store in refrigerator until ready to use.

Cumin-Carrot Oil

1 cup unflavored oil
4 tbsp cumin seed, toasted
4 carrots, cut into small chunks
Salt and pepper to taste

Put carrots, cumin, and oil in a blender. Puree until liquid.

Add salt and pepper to taste. Store in refrigerator until ready to use. Strain.

Korean Braised Short Ribs

One of the most famous and loved recipes from Korea is Grilled Short Ribs. Here is our version of braised short ribs with the most tender meat you have ever tasted. This recipe doesn't disappoint. The cooking technique creates a lot of rich, meaty flavor and it is what I consider the ultimate comfort food.

Serves 4

4 lbs short ribs
All-purpose flour
Salt and pepper to taste
Cayenne pepper
Unflavored oil for searing
2 cups onion, chopped
1 cup carrots
2 tbsp tomato paste
½ cup sugar
¼ cup sesame oil
6 green onions, chopped
10 cloves garlic
2 cups red wine of your choice
1 cup soy sauce
½ cup mirin*
3 cups stock
Long beans or green beans
Watercress or spinach
Butter for finishing

Dust short ribs with salt, pepper, and cayenne. Coat with flour. Sear each piece on all sides. Add onions, carrots, and tomato paste, and brown. Deglaze with wine and sauces. Add sugar, sesame oil, green onions, garlic, and stock. Simmer for 2 hours, or until short ribs are tender. Correct seasoning. Let sit in refrigerator overnight for best flavor. Strain out all cooking liquid, and reserve meat. Sauté beans and greens in butter. Add liquid and meat. Bring up to boil, serve with rice and fresh watercress or spinach.

*Note: Mirin is a sweetened rice vinegar. Check for it in the Asian aisle of your local grocer.

Shaken Beef

Shaken beef is a staple in Vietnamese cuisine. The translation means "beef cooked like dice." When you are cooking this dish in a wok or fry pan, the technique for cooking the beef is like shaking dice. The beef is tender and good for any occasion.

Serves 2

16 oz filet, cut into cubes
2 cloves garlic, crushed
Sugar, salt and pepper to taste
Unflavored oil, for frying
1 bunch green onion, cut into 2 inch pieces
1 red onion, slivered
½ bunch watercress
Fried shallot, for garnish
1 tbsp rice wine vinegar
1 tsp sugar
1 tbsp rice wine
2 tbsp light soy sauce
1 tsp fish sauce
2 tbsp stock
1 tbsp freshly squeezed lime juice

Mint Oil

1 bunch mint, blanched
½ cup spinach, blanched
1 cup unflavored oil

Puree all items in blender. Puree until smooth.

Cut filet into cubes. Marinate in garlic, sugar, salt, and pepper for 1 hour in the refrigerator.

Prepare vegetables.

In a hot wok, sear steak cubes. Add red and green onions, and sauces. Add watercress, and toss until beef is medium rare, about 2 minutes.

Serve on plate with steamed rice. Drizzle with mint oil. Garnish with freshly fried or store-bought fried shallots.

HONEY SOY SEARED AHI TUNA

When asked about why our tuna is so good, the one word answer is "fresh." I'm pretty tough on our distributors, by demanding high-quality products. It's worth it in the end because we get numerous compliments on our fish.

Our tuna recipe is simple. Finish it off with a honey and soy sauce so that it clings to the tuna for great additional flavor.

Serves 4

4-8 oz pieces of tuna
5 oz honey
3 oz soy sauce
Unflavored oil, for searing
Salt and pepper to taste

Heat pan to high heat. Season each piece of tuna with salt and pepper. Coat tuna with oil.

Sear on all sides of tuna. Add soy and honey to the pan. Simmer for 2 minutes, and remove tuna from pan. Cut into slices and serve with sauce from pan.

Serve steamed jasmine rice and quick-sautéed vegetables with this dish. Drizzle with a little Cilantro Oil for an added touch of sophisticated color and flavor.

Cilantro Oil
½ bunch cilantro
1 cup unflavored oil
Salt and pepper to taste

Clean and dry the cilantro. Put leaves into blender. Add salt and pepper. Drizzle oil into moving blender. Oil will keep for 1 week in the refrigerator.

Rama Thai Delight

Rama Delight was created for the current reign of kings in Thailand. If you love peanuts, then this recipe is for you. You'll be surprised what little effort it takes to have such a rich, deeply flavored Thai dish.

Serves 2

1 lb shrimp, cleaned and de-veined, chicken or beef, sliced
1 bunch spinach or broccoli
3 tbsp crushed peanuts
1 tbsp red curry paste
½ cup coconut milk
1 tbsp fish sauce
1 tbsp unflavored oil

Heat pan. Add oil and curry paste. Sauté about 3 minutes to cook out raw flavor. Add meat, sauté until almost done, then add coconut milk, fish sauce, and spinach.

Finish with peanuts.

Serve with steamed Jasmine Rice.
(see page 130)

COCONUT CHICKEN STIR FRY

You may think that coconut milk is a naturally occurring product; however, it is really an infusion of shredded coconut flesh and water. The cooking and boiling process creates the coconut milk. This recipe is very simple to make and has a delicious and delightful coconut flavor. Try cooking with your senses and add any fresh vegetables or seasonings that you like.

Serves 2

12 oz unsweetened coconut milk
1 tbsp fish sauce
1 stalk lemongrass, chopped
8 oz chicken, sliced
Unflavored oil, for sautéing
½ cup bok choy or broccoli, chopped
¼ cup carrots, shredded
¼ cup peppers, chopped
8-10 straw mushrooms
Salt and pepper to taste
Toasted coconut for garnish

Heat oil in pan. Add chicken and sauté until almost done. Add vegetables and liquids. Bring to a boil. Plate with steamed rice and drizzle with Cilantro-Peanut Oil. Sprinkle toasted coconut for garnish.

Cilantro-Peanut Oil Drizzle

½ bunch cilantro
½ cup freshly roasted peanuts
1 cup unflavored oil
Salt and pepper to taste

Clean and dry cilantro. Put leaves into blender. Add peanuts and salt. Drizzle oil into moving blender. Oil will keep for 1 week in the refrigerator.

INDIAN RED BUTTER CHICKEN

Our Indian Red Butter Chicken has the flavors of ginger and tomato. If you can afford it, buy a tandoori oven to roast your chicken. For the rest of us, just roast it in your regular oven or throw it on the grill. You'll want to sop up the sauce with some Indian flatbread or soak it all in your basmati rice.

Serves 4

1½ lbs tomatoes
2 tbsp ginger
4 chiles, seeded
2 tsp ground coriander
Salt and pepper to taste
½ cup fresh cilantro
4 grilled, roasted, or fried chicken breasts
¼ cup butter
¼ cup cream
½ cup peas, fresh or frozen
½ cup onions, sliced

Cook tomatoes, ginger, chiles, onions, and coriander in saucepan until reduced by half. Puree mixture until smooth. Add cream, peas, and fold in butter. Taste for seasoning.

Sauce chicken and garnish with cilantro. Serve with steamed basmati rice or Indian flatbread and Cumin-Coriander Raita.

Cumin-Coriander Raita

1 cup plain yogurt
1 tbsp toasted cumin
1 tbsp toasted coriander
1 European cucumber,* shredded
Salt and pepper to taste

Combine all ingredients. Store in refrigerator until ready to use.

*Note: European Cucumber is also known as a hot-house or seedless cucumber. They are available at your local market.

HONEY SOY GLAZED BURGER

This Honey Soy Glaze can be used on fish or chicken. However, it is delicious on a hamburger and can be easily prepared with ingredients you may already have in the pantry. We made these for the first time at a catered barbeque party. We actually ran out and had to hurry & make more! Luckily we pulled it off without a hitch.

Serves 4

2 lbs ground chuck
Salt and pepper to taste
½ lb butter
2 tbsp fresh chopped herbs
3 tbsp honey
3 tbsp soy sauce
Lettuce, tomato slices
8 slices pepper jack cheese
4 buns of your choice

Combine butter and herbs in bowl. Shape into a log and refrigerate. Cut log into 1½ oz pieces. Make a patty to fit your selected bun. Burger should weigh about ½ lb. Stuff herbed butter in middle of patty. Grill each patty on high heat in hot pan or over open flame. To get proper grill marks, turn patty ¼ turn after 1 minute of cooking. Cook for another minute, and flip burger once. Cook to desired temperature. Brush burger with honey and soy sauce. Grill or toast bun. Spread remaining herbed butter on buns. Top patties with pepper jack cheese, lettuce, and tomato.

CHINESE CHAR-SIU ROASTED PORK LOIN

Char-Siu is originally from Southeastern China and the name translates as "fork-roasted." We take a classic BBQ sauce and marinate our pork loin, and then roast it. We serve this dish with Walnut Fried Rice (see page 134) and extra BBQ sauce on the plate.

Serves 4

4-6 oz pork tenderloins
⅔ cup hoisin sauce
4 tbsp soy sauce
2 tbsp rice wine
2 tbsp ketchup
4 tbsp sugar

Combine all ingredients. Marinate for 2 hours.

Grill or sear all sides of loins.

Bring remaining marinade to a boil.

Baste pork with boiled marinade and place in 350°F oven until internal temperature of meat reaches 145°F.

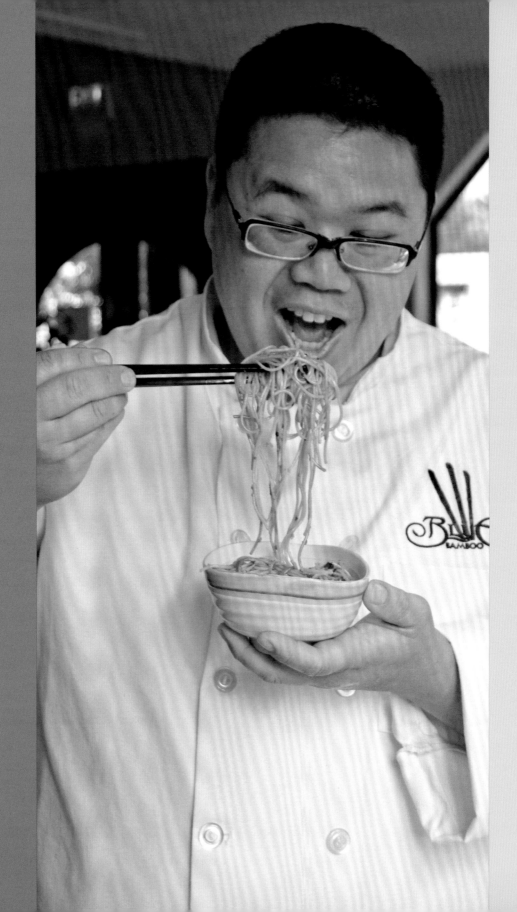

MEIN STREET

We could have easily called this section "Noodles and Rice." We thought it deserved a name that is much more fun. Many years ago, my family had a restaurant on Main Street in Jacksonville, Florida, called Little Dragon. We never called that restaurant by its name and simply called it "Main Street." So now, we're calling this section of the book, which is dedicated to Lo Mein, Pad Thai, and Fried Rice, "Mein Street."

CLASSIC PAD THAI

It's easy to judge a Thai restaurant by its version of Pad Thai, the national noodle dish of Thailand. Before we opened *Blue Bamboo*, I went to my friend's restaurant in Atlanta to learn her version of this dish. They have won many local awards for their Pad Thai, and you can taste why. Making Pad Thai sounds difficult, but it's really pretty easy. It takes a little planning ahead, but the actual cooking time is less than 5 minutes.

Serves 4

1-8 oz package medium or small Pad Thai rice noodles, soaked in water overnight
½ lb shrimp or chicken (optional)
1 egg
2 tbsp fish sauce
3 tbsp white vinegar
3 tbsp sugar
1 tbsp ketchup
½ tbsp paprika
1 tbsp unflavored oil, for stir frying
1 tbsp garlic, smashed
¼ cup chopped scallions
½ cup bean sprouts
¼ cup roasted peanuts
Lime wedges for garnish

Place oil in hot wok or pan. Add garlic and scallions. Sauté until fragrant. Add egg and chicken or shrimp and cook until almost done. Add in noodles, vinegar, ketchup, fish sauce, sugar, and paprika. Add bean sprouts and stir. Cook until noodles are soft. Sprinkle peanuts in noodles. Garnish with lime wedges.

VIETNAMESE COCONUT-CURRY RICE NOODLES WITH DUCK

Here is our most creative noodle recipe, which is made with curry powder. Curry powder is a great blend of approximately 20 dried spices. Turmeric is the main spice in the mixture that gives curry its gorgeous green and gold color. You'll know curry when you smell it. It is pungent and fragrant at the same time.

Serves 4

12 oz dried rice noodles, re-hydrated
1 tbsp unflavored oil, for stir frying
½ tsp ginger, minced
½ tsp garlic, minced
1 tbsp scallions
1 cup sliced onions
½ cup shredded carrots
1 cup chicken broth
⅓ cup coconut milk
1 tbsp fish sauce
1½ tsp sugar
1 lb rice noodles, re-hydrated
1 tbsp curry powder
1 duck breast, roasted and cut into thin slices
Fresh herbs for garnish

Soak rice noodles in warm water for 20 minutes. Drain and set aside.

Heat oil in wok. Add ginger, garlic, and scallion. Add curry powder, and onions. Sauté to release aroma and cook until onions are almost done. Add coconut milk and chicken broth. Bring to a boil. Add sugar and fish sauce. Stir and add noodles and duck. Serve immediately after noodles are warmed throughout. Garnish with fresh herbs.

GREEN CURRY SHRIMP LO MEIN

This pasta dish is reminiscent of one I made while in culinary school. Since then I have made hundreds of orders of this pasta at the restaurant. The Lo Mein is a little tart from the lime juice in this recipe, and very fragrant from the green curry paste, which is a blend of spices and fresh herbs.

Serves 2

2 tbsp coconut milk
2 tbsp fish sauce
2 tbsp lime juice
2 tbsp green curry paste*
¼ cup chives
¼ cup bean sprouts
½ cup snow peas, blanched
½ lb shrimp, grilled
½ cup carrots, shredded
1 lb lo mein egg noodles, cooked

Blanch snow peas and cook pasta. Set aside.

In a wok, bring fish sauce, lime juice, curry paste, and coconut milk to a boil.

Add the noodles, vegetables, and shrimp.

Toss to coat until heated.

Garnish with a slice of lime.

*Note: Green curry paste is available in your local Asian market.

Shrimp Nasi Goreng (Fried rice)

For years, my Indonesian aunt made fried rice for family gatherings. The technique is basically Chinese, but here we use sweet soy, also known as Kecap Manis as a seasoning. We like finishing this recipe with peanuts.

Serves 2 as a main dish, 4 as a side

½ cup shrimp, peeled and de-veined
¼ cup scallions, chopped
¼ cup red onion, sliced
¼ cup carrots, shredded
½ cup bean sprouts
¼ cup lettuce, shredded
2 cups long grain rice, cooked and cooled
1 egg
1 tbsp unflavored oil, for frying
½ tsp salt
½ tsp pepper
1 tbsp Kecap Manis*
2 tbsp soy sauce
Crushed peanuts and cilantro sprigs for garnish

Start with cold, cooked rice.

Heat a non-stick pan to medium heat. Add oil. Break an egg into the hot oil. Swirl it around to cook. Add onions. Cook for about 2 minutes. Add shrimp and scallions. Add cold rice and stir, toasting all sides of each grain. Add carrots and bean sprouts.

Season with salt, pepper, and soy sauces. Stir. Be careful, rice will want to stick to pan.

Garnish with sliced green onions, cilantro, lettuce, and peanuts.

*Note: Kecap Manis is a sweet soy sauce that is widely used in Indonesian cooking. It is a thick, richly colored sauce that can be found at your local Asian market.

BLUE BAMBOO CHICKEN PAD THAI

When we opened *Blue Bamboo*, this was the only version of Pad Thai that we served. I wanted to take the classic flavors of Pad Thai that everyone loves, and do our own interpretation of it. Our version adds coconut milk and red curry paste to give it a slightly richer flavor than classic Pad Thai.

Serves 4

8 oz package rice noodles, large flat size,
   soaked overnight
8 oz chicken breast, strips
1 oz unflavored oil
1 oz garlic minced
1 oz ginger, minced
1 tsp red curry paste
½ oz scallion, green parts only
¼ cup each red, green and yellow peppers,
   julienned
½ cup bean sprouts
½ tbsp sugar
2 tbsp fish sauce
½ cup coconut milk
2 tbsp white vinegar
4 tbsp roasted peanuts, chopped
Cilantro, coarsely chopped for garnish

Heat oil in wok. Add ginger, garlic, chicken, and scallion. Cook until almost done. Add vegetables and cook until tender. Combine other ingredients except noodles in wok. Heat thoroughly. Add noodles and toss to coat. Heat through.

Plate and garnish with peanuts and cilantro.

UDON WITH TEMPURA VEGETABLES

The hearty part of this dish, which can be found at any traditional Japanese restaurant, is thick, chewy Udon noodles. Classically, the noodles are served in a soup. Here, we make a stir fry and top with Tempura vegetables. My mother and I always order Tempura vegetables as an appetizer when we go to Japanese restaurants. This basic recipe for Tempura is easy. Eat the vegetables soon after they are out of the fryer, while they are still warm and crispy.

Serves 2

Tempura

1 egg
1 cup cold soda water
1 cup all-purpose flour
Salt to taste
Oil for deep frying
1 cup vegetables, blanched
Substitutions: use any seasonal vegetables, chicken or shrimp

Prepare all ingredients for battering.
Thinly sliced items will cook quickly.
Combine egg, cold soda water, and flour.
Heat oil to 350°F.

Dip items in batter and fry until slightly golden.
Season with salt while items are still slightly wet.

Noodles

1 tbsp unflavored oil, for pan frying
¼ cup mirin*
¼ cup soy sauce
8 oz fresh udon noodles, cooked
2 tbsp butter

Heat pan. Add oil and Udon noodles. Stir until heated throughout. Add vegetables, mirin, and soy sauce. Stir until thoroughly heated. Finish with butter and serve with fried vegetables.

*Note: Mirin is a sweetened rice vinegar. Check for it in the Asian aisle of your local grocer.

CANTONESE CHOW MEIN
PAN-FRIED NOODLE WITH SHRIMP

Egg noodles are one of my childhood favorite foods. Our recipe has a texture combination of crispy and soft and has a classic Cantonese ginger-soy flavor. My grandfather used to call this noodle dish by its Chinese name, "two-seared faces." When my cousin was little, she translated it as "two seared heads." From that point on, our family always jokingly called it "two seared heads." Whatever you want to call it, it's good, and worth the effort to make.

Serves 2

1-8 oz package fresh egg noodles,* cooked and drained
1 cup bean sprouts
1 tsp ginger, minced
1 tsp garlic, minced
1 tsp scallions
½ cup carrots
8 oz shrimp or pork, sliced
1 cup stock
1 tbsp soy sauce
1 tsp sesame oil
2 tbsp unflavored oil, for pan frying and sautéing
Salt and pepper to taste

In a non-stick pan, heat noodles with 1 tbsp oil until crispy. Flip over, and brown second side. Set aside.

In wok, heat remaining unflavored oil. Add ginger, garlic, and scallion. Stir until fragrant. Add shrimp and sauté until done. Add carrots, bean sprouts, and stock.

Season with soy sauce, sesame oil, salt, and pepper. Pour over pan-fried noodles.

*Note: You can find fresh egg noodles at your local grocer.

RIVER RICE NOODLES WITH BEEF

These River Rice Noodles are a traditional finish to a dim-sum brunch. One of our good customers and friends comes in for this dish twice a week. In a small town like ours, it is hard to find these noodles. However, it is not too hard to make them yourself. The chewy texture of these noodles is comforting, and the flavor in the gingery brown sauce is addictive.

Serves 2

1 tbsp ginger, minced
1 tbsp garlic, minced
1 lb fresh rice noodles
1 cup bean sprouts
½ cup carrots, shredded
½ cup onions, sliced
1 tbsp soy sauce
3 tbsp oyster sauce
⅓ lb beef, sliced
¼ cup scallion tops
Salt and pepper to taste
2 tbsp unflavored oil, for stir frying

Heat oil in wok. Add onions and beef. Stir fry until almost done. Add ginger and garlic. Stir until fragrant. Add noodles, carrots, and bean sprouts. Season with salt, pepper, soy, and oyster sauces. Add scallion. Stir until warmed through.

Fresh Steamed Rice Noodles

1 cup rice flour
½ cup corn starch
2 cups water
1 tsp salt

Combine ingredients. Spread ⅛ inch thick layer on a flat pan and steam. Remove after 3 minutes, and cool. Roll into tubes. Cut into ½ inch wide noodles.

SINGAPORE STREET NOODLES

This has always been one of my favorite noodle dishes with abundant curry flavor. There's something about these thin rice noodles that is satisfying and extraordinary. Add more chile paste if you really like it spicy.

Serves 2

8 oz package thin rice noodles, re-hydrated
2 tbsp soy sauce
1 tbsp curry powder
½ cup carrots, shredded
½ cup onions, sliced
2 eggs
½ cup scallions
1 tbsp unflavored oil
1 tbsp garlic chile paste
Salt and pepper to taste
Chicken stock, as needed

Soak noodles in warm water, for 15 minutes. Drain and set aside.

Heat 1 tablespoon of oil in wok or sauté pan. Add eggs. Stir fry until solid. Add onions and carrots. Fry until onions are almost translucent. Add curry powder and noodles. Stir fry until noodles are heated through. Add scallions and soy sauce and stock to help warm noodles.

Heat through and plate.

Pancit Bihon

When you think of Filipino food, the first dish that comes to mind is Pancit. Jacksonville has a large Filipino community, and every Filipino says their mother makes the best Pancit. Our version is the best that I've had. It's customary to have this dish on birthdays because the noodles symbolize longevity. Eating these noodles will make you happy. I guess you really can't ask for more than a long, happy life.

Serves 4

8 oz thin rice stick noodles, re-hydrated
1 tbsp unflavored oil
1 tbsp minced garlic
1 onion, sliced
1 cup cabbage, shredded
1 carrot, shredded
½ cup celery, shredded
1 cup cooked shrimp
½ cup roasted chicken, pulled
¼ cup fish sauce
1 cup stock
Salt and pepper to taste
1 green onion, slivered
Lime wedges or sour oranges for garnish

Soak noodles in warm water for 20 minutes. Drain and set aside. Cut into 2-inch strips.

Heat oil. Add garlic and sauté until fragrant. Add onion, cabbage, carrot, and celery. Add shrimp, chicken, fish sauce, and stock. Stir in rice stick noodles and season with salt and pepper to taste. Cook until all liquid has been absorbed by noodles. Sprinkle with green onion and garnish with lime or sour orange.

Vietnamese Bun Noodle

When I think of quintessential Vietnamese comfort food, I think of this noodle recipe. In any big Vietnamese community, you can find dozens of restaurants that serve their own versions of Bun (boon). This dish has a satisfying combination of sweet, salty, and sour nuances. Only use the freshest herbs.

Serves 2

8 oz thin rice noodles, re-hydrated
½ cup Thai basil
½ cup carrots, shredded
¼ cup cucumber, shredded
1 cup lettuce, shredded
¼ cup cilantro sprigs
½ cup fresh bean sprouts
Chives for garnish
¼ cup roasted peanuts, crushed
Fried shallots for garnish

Re-hydrate rice noodles in warm water for 20 minutes. Drain and set aside.

Arrange remaining ingredients on noodles in bowl.

Serve with nuoc cham dipping sauce.

Nuoc Cham Dipping Sauce

¼ cup fish sauce
¼ cup rice wine vinegar
½ lime, juiced
2 tbsp brown sugar
1 tsp garlic, minced
2 tbsp stock
¼ cup carrots, shredded
1 tsp chile, sliced

Bring all ingredients except carrots and chiles to a boil. Let cool.

Add carrots and chiles for garnish.

SHIRATAKI

Shirataki is a root vegetable noodle that is great for staying healthy. It has protein from added soy flour, and is low in bad carbohydrates. On its own, it has very little flavor. When we bump it up with Vietnamese Nuoc Mam fish sauce and fresh herbs, it becomes a flavorful and healthy dish. Nuoc Mam is the base for Nuoc Cham, the sauce we make for our Vietnamese Bun Noodle. It is made from anchovies, and it is extremely pungent, but it adds a nice richness to any dish.

Serves 2

1-8 oz package tofu Shirataki noodles
1 cup mixed vegetables, sliced
3 cups flavorful broth
2 tbsp fish sauce

Fresh Thai basil, sprigs
Scallion greens, slivered
Jalapeno peppers, sliced
Cilantro, sprigs

Make a flavorful broth. We like to use chicken bones, beef bones, and aromatics. When I say aromatics, I mean parsley, onions, carrots, and celery. Cover ingredients in stock pot with water. Bring to a boil. Simmer for 1 hour. Strain and reserve until needed.

Bring broth to a boil, and reduce to a simmer. Add meat if desired and cook until done. Add vegetables and fish sauce. Open shirataki package and strain. Place noodles into broth. Garnish soup with basil, scallions, cilantro, and jalapeno peppers.

BEEF WONTON RAVIOLIS

Here is our *Hip* way of making fresh Raviolis. Save time by purchasing pre-prepared wonton skins. Try our tomato sauce recipe or use your own. An Italian cookbook author once told me that Asian food and Italian food are very much alike. In both styles of cooking, the sauce is made in the same pot as the main ingredient. This is why Italian cooking is so familiar to me.

Serves 4

8 oz round wonton wrappers
Beaten egg, for sealing

Filling

8 oz ground chuck
¼ cup onions, finely chopped and sautéed
Salt and pepper to taste
1 tbsp garlic, minced
½ cup Parmesan cheese

Sauce

8 oz tomato sauce
6 oz crushed tomatoes
¼ cup basil
2 tbsp fresh oregano leaves
Salt and pepper to taste
Olive oil and balsamic vinegar, for drizzling on plate

Combine filling ingredients. Set aside.

Place 1 tbsp of filling in the center of each wonton skin.

Fold the dumpling in half and seal the edges with egg. Pinch the corners together. Boil the Ravioli in salted water until they float to the surface. Drain and set aside.

Combine sauce ingredients. Bring to a boil. Reduce to a simmer for 20 minutes.

Serve Raviolis in tomato sauce with fresh basil and balsamic vinegar.

SAKE-MISO RISOTTO

I learned how to make Risotto from a very talented and decorated Italian chef. The most important part of the risotto process is what he called "mantecatura," or mount with butter. It's a way of incorporating your butter vigorously into the rice at the end to add extra creaminess to the dish. The Risotto is a great side dish. Try adding any seasonal vegetables such as mushrooms, squash, or carrots and it quickly becomes a delicious vegetarian meal.

Serves 4 as a side

2 cups medium grain Arborio rice
2 tbsp golden miso
8 cups stock, heated
2 tbsp unflavored oil
½ cup chopped onion
½ cup sake, heated
2 tbsp butter, in chunks
Salt and pepper to taste

Cook onion in unflavored oil over medium heat. Add rice to pot and stir to toast rice grains. Add miso, onions, and sake. Add heated broth, ½ cup at a time until all broth is absorbed, approx. 20 minutes. Mount Risotto with butter off the heat just before serving.

Risotto Wontons

8 oz pack wonton wrappers
Egg, for sealing
2 cups cold Risotto, cooked
Salt and pepper to taste
¼ cup Parmesan cheese
¼ cup butter
Heated oil, for frying

Mix Risotto with butter and cheese. Season with salt and pepper, if necessary.

Seal 1 tbsp of filling in a wonton skin with egg. Fry in 350°F oil until wontons float. Drain on paper towels.

Serve with shaved Parmesan cheese and a touch of balsamic vinegar.

EASY JASMINE RICE

In Chinese, one way to greet people is to ask them if they've eaten yet. The literal translation of that phrase is "Have you eaten rice yet?" Eating rice is such a big part of Asian culture. Jasmine rice is served with many of our meals. It is fragrant, warm, and soul soothing. Here's a sure-fire way to get perfect rice anytime.

Serves 4

2 cups Jasmine Rice
3 cups water (approximate, use knuckle* measurement)

Rinse rice until liquid is almost clear. Cover rice with water in a 2 quart saucepan and fill to first notch above index finger over rice. Bring to boil. Reduce to low and heat for 20 minutes, covered. Take off heat. Let sit, covered, for 15 minutes. Fluff with fork.

*Note: For cooking rice, an easy way to tell if you have enough water in your pot is to place your fingertip just so that it is touching the top of the rice. Fill water until the water level just reaches your knuckle. That will give you just enough water to make sure the rice kernels are completely cooked.

KABOCHA SQUASH WONTONS

My father recently retired from his work of 36 years with the state health department. When his colleagues asked what he was going to do with all of his time, he said, "Plant a garden." That's just what he did. He started growing corn, melons, peanuts, and this funny squash called Kabocha. I had eaten this squash in California and enjoyed it, and I was happy to see my father growing Kabocha. You can find this squash commercially in specialty markets and Asian Markets. It tastes like acorn squash or butternut squash, and it is a natural filling for pasta.

Serves 4

1 pack wonton wrappers
Egg, for sealing

1 Kabocha squash, halved and roasted with
   salt and pepper
Salt and pepper to taste
½ cup Parmesan cheese
¼ cup butter
Salted water, for boiling

3 cups seasoned rich broth
1 tbsp five-spice powder
Salt and pepper to taste
Scallion greens, slivered

Roast squash in oven, flesh side down, until done (about 30 minutes, 350°F).

Let cool. Mix with butter and cheese. Season with salt and pepper.

Seal 1 tbsp of filling in each dumpling. Fold edges over, making sure the seal is tight. Boil dumplings until they float.

Serve with warmed broth, seasoned with five-spice powder and salt and pepper. Garnish with scallions.

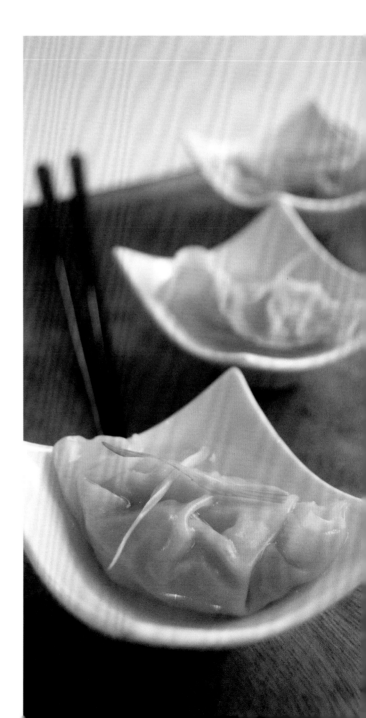

LAKSA CURRIED COCONUT NOODLES

This dish is found in Singapore, Indonesia, and Malaysia. Laksa is a curried noodle soup that is usually spicy and has layers of flavor from various combinations of spices. It's a street food in Southeast Asia and you can find many vendors selling their own versions. When in Asia, look for the vendor with the longest line. It will be worth the wait.

Serves 4

2 tbsp red curry paste
1 tsp soy sauce
1 tsp fresh ginger, minced
½ tsp fresh garlic, minced
1 tbsp oil, for stir frying
1 tsp turmeric, ground
1 tsp sugar
1 tbsp tamarind paste
½ lb thick noodles, cooked
8 oz cooked chicken, pulled
8 oz shrimp, cooked
2 cups chicken stock
½ cup carrot, mandolined
¼ cup fish sauce
1 cup coconut milk
Sambal* or garlic-chile hot sauce to taste

Garnish
Chiles, sliced
Cucumber, julienned
Bean sprouts
¼ cup cilantro leaves, chopped
¼ cup Thai basil, chopped

Heat oil in a large saucepan over medium high heat and stir in red curry paste, soy sauce, ginger, garlic, turmeric, sugar, and tamarind paste. Sauté until fragrant.

Add chicken stock and bring to a boil. Reduce heat, stir in herbs and fish sauce, and simmer for 5 minutes. Stir in the coconut milk and bring to a simmer.

Divide the noodles, chicken, carrots, and shrimp among serving bowls. Arrange garnishes on top. Pour sauce over bowls.

*Note: Sambal is a chunky Southeast Asian chile garlic condiment used to spice up any food. It's red and contains chile seeds.

TOASTED WALNUT FRIED RICE

This recipe won me a trip to Napa Valley when I was a culinary student. It's a sophisticated recipe, but what's most important is that it tastes fabulous! There is something about the combination of sherry and walnuts that is delightful, comfortable, and enjoyable.

Serves 2

3 cups cooked long-grain rice
¾ cup walnut pieces
1 cup medium-bodied sherry, for reduction
¼ cup red peppers, diced
¼ cup green peppers, diced
1 tbsp unflavored oil
¼ cup onion, finely diced
2 tbsp oyster sauce
Chicken stock as needed
Salt and pepper to taste
4 tbsp walnut oil
¼ bunch chives, ¾ inch lengths, or green onions (scallions)

Make rice: see Easy Jasmine Rice, on page 130 for technique.

Spread on sheet pan and place in refrigerator for at least 2 hours. (Cook rice the night before and refrigerate for best results.)

Toast walnuts until golden brown, 12-15 minutes, on clean sheet pan in 350°F oven. Remove and pour walnuts on another sheet pan to cool.

Reduce 1 cup sherry to a syrupy consistency, yielding about ¼ cup of reduction.

Heat wok. Add unflavored oil and finely diced onions to wok. Add peppers and stir fry for 2 minutes. Add cooled rice and oyster sauce. Stir fry until thoroughly coated and heated. Re-hydrate rice with chicken stock as needed in wok. Salt and pepper to taste. Add walnuts and stir to distribute evenly.

Drizzle sherry reduction and walnut oil on outside perimeter of rice. Sprinkle with chives.

PEANUT-PESTO NOODLE SALAD

This is a quick lunch noodle salad that can be made ahead of time and packed for tailgating or picnics. Believe it or not, peanut flavor with basil is a great combination. There are a lot of ingredients, but this salad is easy to make. Try the noodle salad served warmed as a main dish.

Serves 4 as a side course

1 lb pasta, cooked until al dente
1 cup fresh cilantro
1 cup basil, blanched
½ cup peanuts, roasted
2 tbsp garlic, minced
1 tbsp ginger, minced
½ cup soy sauce
¼ cup scallions, shredded
1 red pepper, chopped
2 carrots, shredded
2 tbsp chopped peanuts, for garnish
Salt and pepper to taste

Boil pasta until al dente. Shock in ice water to stop cooking. Drain.

In a food processor, pulse basil and cilantro with peanuts. Add ginger, garlic, and soy sauce. Refrigerate until ready to use.

Mix remaining ingredients with pasta. Season with salt and pepper. Toss pasta with desired amount of Pesto.

Serve in rice bowls with chopsticks.

Couscous

Couscous is one of those funny things that you see everywhere, and it is a mystery to most what it is. Couscous is a rolled and steamed semolina flour that comes in 2 main sizes. My first experience with Couscous was at a Moroccan restaurant. Since then, I've enjoyed watching people try it for the first time. There is always a look of hesitancy at first, followed by an expression of delight when the person tries Couscous. You can flavor Couscous however you like. Be creative. We have even flavored Couscous with foie gras for a super rich indulgence. Here is how to make both kinds:

Serves 4 as a side course

Israeli Pearl Couscous

1 tbsp olive oil
¾ lb pearl couscous
1¾ cups chicken broth
1 cup water
¼ tsp crumbled saffron threads

Heat oil in a heavy saucepan over medium heat. Toast Couscous in pan until golden, about 3 to 5 minutes. Add broth, water, and saffron to Couscous and bring to a simmer. Cover until liquid is absorbed and Couscous is al dente, about 10 to 12 minutes. Let stand covered for 10 minutes.

Toss with your favorite vinaigrette and herbs. Serve at room temperature.

Basic Couscous

1 cup couscous
1 tbsp olive oil
1¼ cups stock
¼ cup raisins
¼ cup almonds, toasted
¼ cup red pepper, diced
Salt and pepper to taste

Bring stock to a boil. Add olive oil. Stir in Couscous and cover. Remove from heat. Let stand for 25 minutes. Fluff with fork and toss in raisins, red peppers, and almonds. Season with salt and pepper to taste.

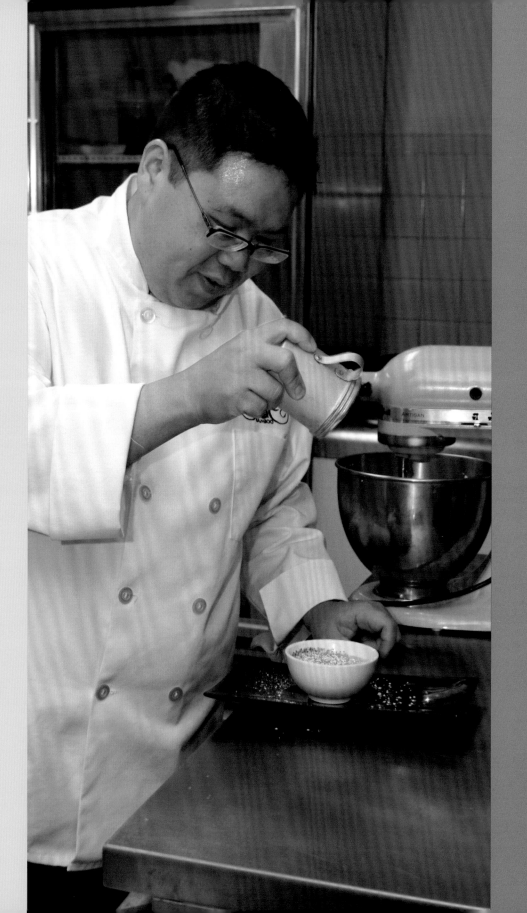

Happy Endings

Every story deserves a happy ending. At *Blue Bamboo*, we believe that just like every great story, every great meal deserves a happy ending.

Note: Baking is an exact science. The best way to guarantee results is by weight. Our baking ingredients are given in ounces and pounds because that eliminates the airspace that is inconsistent when you use volume measures.

CHEWY GOOEY CARAMEL BROWNIE

A friend in New York shared this brownie recipe with me. She made this using one of the best brands of chocolate. The brownies are perfectly chewy, gooey, and very much like a rich chocolate cake. Once you try them, you'll never make any other brownies!

Serves 4

⅔ cup all-purpose flour
¼ tsp salt
½ tsp baking powder
6 oz chocolate, premium brand, semi-sweet
10 tbsp unsalted butter
1⅓ cups sugar
2 tsp vanilla extract
3 eggs
Caramel sauce

Preheat oven to 325°F. Keep the sugar separate and stir the rest of the dry ingredients together in small bowl. Line 8x8 pan with parchment paper so that the brownies will release easily. Melt chocolate and butter in medium bowl, over simmering water. Whisk in the sugar and add vanilla off heat. Whisk in the eggs, one at a time until the batter is smooth and glossy. And add the flour, salt, and baking powder mixture. Mix all ingredients until uniform. Pour into cake pan and drizzle caramel over the brownie batter. Bake at 325°F until toothpick comes out with slight crumbs. Let the brownies cool, and then cut. Serve with caramel sauce and your favorite vanilla ice cream.

Caramel Sauce

1 cup sugar
Water
1 cup milk or heavy cream

Place sugar in heavy bottomed pot. Add just enough water to moisten all grains of sugar. Simmer over medium heat until color begins to turn caramel. Remove from heat and add 1 cup warmed milk or heavy cream. Set aside until needed.

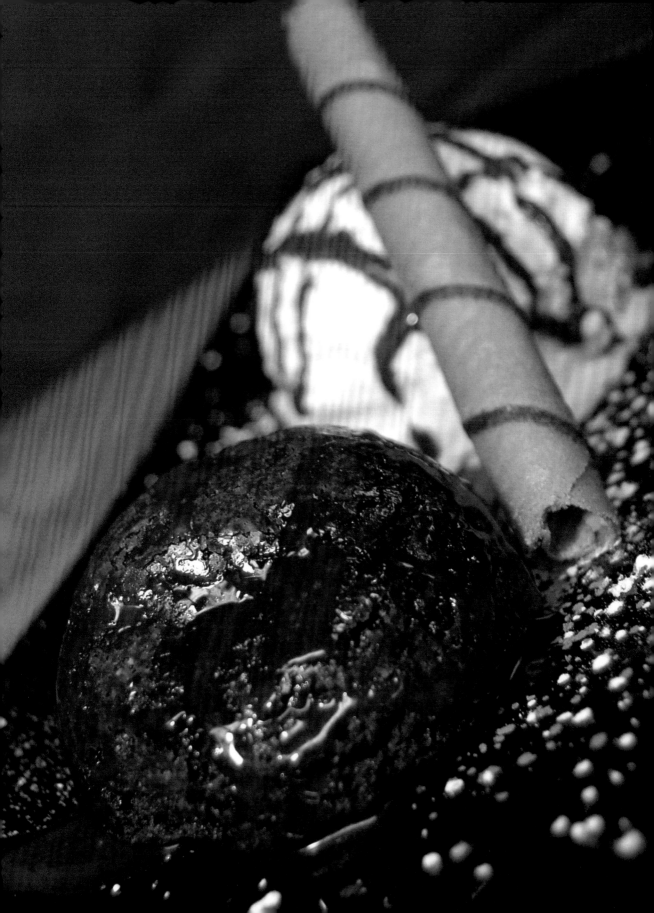

MANDARIN ORANGE CAKE

This is our signature dessert at *Blue Bamboo*. Our servers tell me there is never any left on the plate. A friend inspired me to create this recipe after she ordered a version of it for my birthday a few years ago. The pineapple cream cheese frosting takes this cake over the top, and the mandarin orange layers keep the cake moist.

Serves 10

Sponge Cake

5½ cups cake flour, sifted
5 tsp baking powder
½ tsp salt
¾ lb unsalted butter
3 cups sugar
8 eggs
2 tsp orange extract
16 oz mandarin oranges, crushed and drained, liquid reserved

Preheat oven to 350°F. Sift dry ingredients together. Set aside.

Cream butter and sugar together. Add the eggs, one at a time. Add the orange extract.

Slowly add the dry ingredients and incorporate for 3 minutes. Add the mandarin oranges slowly, until entire 16 oz is evenly distributed. Separate batter evenly between three floured 8-inch cake pans. Always place a piece of parchment paper in the bottom so that the cake will release easily. Bake the cake for 20 minutes or until a toothpick comes out crumb free.

Pineapple Cream Cheese Frosting

1 lb unsalted butter
1 lb cream cheese
½ lb powdered sugar
1 tsp orange extract
8 oz can crushed pineapple, strained

Cream the butter and sugar together. Add the cream cheese 1 oz at a time while the mixer is still on. Add the orange extract and pineapple, combining well.

Re-moisten each layer with mandarin orange syrup or orange juice.

*Note: Our mandarin orange cake is garnished with an almond tuile cookie. Please see recipe on page 164.

GREEN TEA CREAM PUFFS

I went on a one-day food trip to New York recently, and visited 2 Japanese shops that make cream puffs exclusively. Each of the shops featured various flavors, and here's one that made an exciting combination. The technique is simple for cream puffs and easy to prepare. The shell is a twice-cooked dough. The first cooking is on a stove top, and the second cooking in done when the dough puffs are in the oven. Make sure you dry out the shells well in the oven. A soggy cream puff just isn't as good as a crispy, fresh-filled one.

Makes 8 puffs

Green Tea Pastry Cream

3 egg yolks
⅓ cup sugar
3 tbsp cornstarch
1 cup heavy cream
2 tbsp matcha green tea powder
Pinch salt
2 tbsp butter

Whisk together the egg yolks, ½ of the sugar, and cornstarch. Bring the cream and green tea powder to a boil with salt and remainder of sugar. Add to the yolk mixture slowly. Return to pot and heat mixture slowly until thickened, stirring with a wooden spoon. Cover with plastic wrap so that no skin forms. Refrigerate until ready to use.

Puffs

1 cup milk
4 tbsp butter
⅛ tsp salt
1 tsp sugar
1 cup flour
5 eggs

Preheat oven to 400°F. Bring liquid ingredients to a boil. Stir in the salt and sugar. Add flour in at once and stir rapidly with a spoon on heat until dough leaves sides of the pan. Remove dough and let cool slightly. Put in food processor or stand mixer and add eggs, one at a time to allow eggs to combine completely. Drop spoonfuls of dough onto cookie sheet. Bake for about 25 minutes until golden brown. Cut in half and fill with green tea pastry cream. Sprinkle with powdered sugar and serve.

Peanut Butter Trifle

Peanut Butter Trifles are super rich and incredibly delicious. What makes them so hip is the marbling that I learned from a friend in Orlando. He took two shades of frosting or mousse, and marbled them together. The look was exquisite, and I started presenting our trifles this way.

Serves 8

Peanut Butter Butter Cream

1 lb peanut butter
1 lb butter
1 lb powdered sugar

In stand mixer, whip butter and powdered sugar until light and fluffy. Add peanut butter by the tablespoon, incorporating after each addition.

Set aside.

Thick Chocolate Ganache*

2 cups cream
1 lb chocolate

Bring cream to a boil. Pour over chocolate. Let sit for 5 minutes. Stir until well combined. Refrigerate until cold. Whip in mixer until fluffy, and set aside.

Basic Chocolate Cake

15 oz sugar
9 oz cake flour
¼ oz baking soda
⅔ tsp baking powder
6 oz eggs
10 oz butter, melted
12 oz water
1 tsp vanilla extract
4 oz cocoa powder

Combine dry ingredients and set aside. In a stand mixer, beat eggs, using paddle attachment on mixer at medium speed. Add dry ingredients in thirds, incorporating after each addition. Add butter, water, and vanilla. Mix until smooth batter forms. Bake in your choice of shape at 350°F until toothpick comes out clean. Cool completely before unmolding.

Assembly

Cut cake into thin slices. Place dollup of buttercream and ganache in trifle bowl. Smear to create marbling. Place cake in trifle and repeat marbling. Repeat until trifle bowl is filled.

*Note: Ganache is a chocolate and milk mixture. It can be very thin, like a chocolate sauce, or very thick, like a fudge. The thicker ganaches can be whipped to make a light, airy chocolate mousse.

Vietnamese Coffee Tiramisu

Having worked in an Italian restaurant before I started *Blue Bamboo*, I learned to be an expert on Tiramisu. Vietnamese coffee adds the flavor of chicory to the classic espresso blend. This blend is often called New Orleans Coffee, because that's where it was made so famous. This recipe has a lot of components, but the end result is worth the effort. The Italian translation for Tiramisu is "lift me up," and it certainly does.

Serves 12

1½ lb mascarpone cheese
2 shots chicory coffee espresso
4 oz marsala wine
2 oz heavy cream
1 oz rum
3 oz water
1 tsp vanilla extract
4 eggs, separated
7 oz sugar
1 tbsp unsweetened cocoa powder
1-8 oz package ladyfingers
Cocoa powder, or powdered sugar for garnish

Mix rum, coffee and 3 oz water. Set aside. You will need four bowls for mixing this recipe and then you will combine them all together.

Bowl 1 - Whip yolks over double boiler. Add half of the sugar and half of the marsala. Continue whipping over heat until soft peaks form in approximately 8-10 minutes. Set aside.
Bowl 2 - Heat remaining sugar over double boiler with egg whites and whip until soft peaks form. Set aside.
Bowl 3 - In a cold bowl, whip heavy cream with cocoa powder to full peaks. For best results use a stand mixer.
Bowl 4 - Fold together mascarpone and the remaining marsala wine.

Fold whipped heavy cream into mascarpone mixture. Then fold in whipped egg whites. Finally, combine with whipped marsala yolks.

Soak ladyfingers with all of the coffee mixture. Layer cream mixture with ladyfingers in a bowl, serving glass, or a 9x9 pan. Top with powdered sugar or cocoa powder.

BALSAMIC PEAR BERRY CRUMBLE

At buffet events, we place a portable convection oven on a dessert station and bake these crumbles fresh for our guests. We top each crumble with a scoop of ice cream. Just enough ice cream melts into the crumble before they eat up all the pears and berries!

Serves 8

3 pears, halved, cored and finely chopped
2 pints berries
2 tbsp balsamic vinegar
3 sprigs basil, chopped
7 tbsp sugar
6 tbsp all-purpose flour
¼ lb butter

Preheat the oven to 400°F.

Put the fruit into a bowl with balsamic vinegar, basil, and 2 tbsp of sugar. Add a little more sugar if berries are sour. Mix and put aside.

In a food processor, pulse the flour, butter, and the rest of the sugar to make crumble topping.

Put the fruit into an ovenproof serving dish or ramekins*. Sprinkle the crumble mix over the fruit. Bake for about 30 minutes, or until the top is evenly golden and the fruit has started to bubble up.

Serve with your favorite vanilla ice cream.

*Note: Ramekins are little porcelain crocks that hold oven-baked desserts. You can find them in various sizes at kitchenware stores.

FIVE-SPICED APPLE FRITTERS

Almost every culture has a version of an apple fritter. This is our recipe that is easy, and you'll love the result. It is more apple than fritter and is a great alternative when you don't have time to make Auntie Billie's Apple Pie on page 169. A main ingredient in five-spice powder is cinnamon. The other four spices, together with the cinnamon, add a level of complexity to this dessert.

Serves 6

8 apples, peeled, cored, and cut into wedges
Fresh squeezed lemon juice
2 qts unflavored oil, for frying
2 eggs
⅓ cup milk
1 cup all-purpose flour
1 tsp five-spiced powder
¼ cup sugar
2 tbsp kirsch*
Vanilla ice cream
Cinnamon and powdered sugar for dusting
1 cup balsalmic vinegar, reduced by half, for garnish

Reduce balsalmic vinegar by boiling approximately 20 minutes.

Heat oil to 375°F. Cut apples into 6 wedges. Sprinkle lemon juice over apples to prevent browning.

Whisk together eggs and milk. Add flour, sugar, kirsch, and five-spice powder.

Dip apples in batter and place in hot oil. Fry until golden brown, about 2 minutes.

Plate with ice cream and sprinkle with powdered sugar and cinnamon. Drizzle with balsalmic vinegar reduction.

*Note: Kirsch is cherry flavored brandy that is clear. You can find it in your local liquor store.

EXQUISITE CHOCOLATE WALNUT COOKIES

We make this cookie with my favorite decadent high end chocolate. It's the perfect holiday recipe for a cookie swap. Long ago, there was a cookie shop in a local mall that we went to for this special treat. They grew to a dozen locations around the area, but now there's only one location left, and they've changed the recipe. After some trial and error, here's the recipe I created, and it is as close as I can come to the original. The walnuts are optional in this recipe, but they add a nice texture and give you the nutrients that will put you in a happy mood.

Makes 2 dozen cookies

1 cup butter (2 sticks)
⅓ cup granulated sugar
⅔ cup packed brown sugar
1 tsp vanilla extract
2 large eggs
2 cups all-purpose flour
¼ cup unsweetened cocoa powder
1 tsp baking soda
½ tsp salt
1½ cups chocolate chips
1 cup chopped walnuts

Cream together butter and sugars in mixer. Gradually add eggs and extract. Combine salt, flour, cocoa, and baking soda. Add to butter mixture. Add chips and walnuts at last minute and scoop onto cookie pan. Bake at 350°F for 10 minutes or until desired doneness.

You can make this dough ahead, scoop, and freeze. Then whenever you want cookies, you can have fresh baked ones in less than 15 minutes.

Filipino Banana Cake

A very good customer of ours makes a version of this cake on special occasions. The cake could easily be called the Elvis cake, since his favorite sandwich was peanut butter and banana. It's a natural combination of flavors.

Serves 6

2 cups all-purpose flour
1½ tsp baking powder
1 tsp baking soda
Pinch salt
⅔ cup sugar
½ cup butter
½ cup buttermilk
2 eggs
1 tsp vanilla extract
2 ripe bananas, mashed
½ cup peanuts, roasted and chopped

Topping
½ cup all-purpose flour
½ cup brown sugar
½ cup butter

Preheat oven to 350°F. Combine flour, baking powder, baking soda, salt, and sugar. Add butter and incorporate eggs, buttermilk, and bananas, then vanilla and peanuts.

Stir all ingredients until combined.

For topping, cut brown sugar and butter together with flour.

Fill prepared ramekins almost to top. Sprinkle topping over ramekins.

Bake for 25 minutes or until done. Serve with sliced bananas.

Pinot-Shao Xing Poached Pears

Poached pears are one of the easiest elegant desserts. I made them for some friends who came over for dinner recently. I was pleasantly surprised at the rave reviews. Little did they know how easy these pears were to make. Serve them with a little vanilla ice cream, and reduce the cooking liquid until thick, or syrup-like consistency.

Serves 4

4 pears
2 cups Shao Xing cooking wine*
1 bottle fruity red wine
2 cups sugar
Ginger, orange peel, star anise, and
    cinnamon (optional)

Peel and core pears. Combine wines and sugar in a saucepan with pears and bring to a boil. Simmer for 20 minutes and check with a knife for doneness. Let sit in liquid overnight and cut. Serve with ice cream.

*Note: Shao Xing rice wine is widely used in Chinese cooking. You can find it in your local Asian market.

Egg Jam Crème Brulee

We created this recipe by accident. I was looking for a dessert for our Singapore cooking class and found a mention of Egg Jam, a spread that locals use for toast and crackers. I noticed that the combination of ingredients was close to our classic crème brulee. We took the basic Egg Jam Custard, and made it into a crème brulee. When you prepare this dessert, you will see that it has a nice coconut flavor, and a rich custard texture.

Serves 6

3 cups heavy cream
1 cup coconut milk, unsweetened
9 egg yolks
1 whole egg
1½ cups sugar
1 tbsp vanilla extract

Preheat oven to 350°F. Pour heavy cream and coconut milk into saucepan. Sprinkle ¾ cup sugar on to cream and bring to a boil. Combine remaining sugar with egg and yolks. Slowly drizzle into cream, and add vanilla. Divide into ramekins or bowls, and bake in a water bath for approx. 1 hour. Crème will jiggle slightly when ready.

HIP ASIAN FLAN

Our recipe for Flan is based on my South American friend's recipe, which she learned from her grandmother. We make flan anytime we feel like treating ourselves to Latin flavor. The recipe is easy, and the result will WOW even the toughest flan critic. For this recipe we use a Chinese brand of sweetened condensed milk from Hong Kong. It has a deeper flavor without being gooey, like some of the American brands.

Makes 24 mini flans

2–8 oz cans Chinese sweetened condensed milk
Sugar, as needed for caramel
5 cups whole milk
8 eggs

In a blender, blend milk, eggs, and condensed milk until smooth. Caramelize sugar in sauce pan with water and coat ramekins* with caramel. Fill with mixture and bake in water bath at 325°F about 45 minutes until firmly set. Refrigerate. Run a knife along the edge of ramekin and unmold carefully. The caramel on the bottom of ramekin will help flan release.

*Note: Ramekins are little porcelain crocks that hold oven-baked desserts. You can find them in various sizes at kitchenware stores.

BLACK FOREST CHERRY TORTES

You can find Black Forest Cakes at any local bakery. The combination of cherries, chocolate, and whipped cream is a favorite of many people. Here, we take the classic recipe and plate it individually for a dramatic presentation. For a dinner party, you can make this dessert interactive by setting out all of the components, and letting your guests do the plating themselves. It is fun to see what they create.

Serves 8

Cherries

1 lb pitted cherries, fresh or frozen
½ cup sugar
1 cup water or juice

Stew cherries in sugar, water and liqueur of your choice for 20 minutes.

Whipped Cream

2 tbsp unsweetened cocoa powder (optional)
3 tbsp powdered sugar
2 cups heavy whipping cream

In a very cold mixing bowl, beat all ingredients until soft peaks form. Finish whipping by hand, maintaining cold temperature.

Basic Chocolate Cake

15 oz sugar
9 oz cake flour
¼ oz baking soda
⅔ tsp baking powder
6 oz eggs
10 oz butter, melted
12 oz water
1 tsp vanilla extract
4 oz unsweetened cocoa powder

Combine dry ingredients and set aside. In a stand mixer, Beat eggs, using paddle attachment on mixer at medium speed. Add dry ingredients in thirds, incorporating after each addition. Add butter, water, and vanilla. Mix until a smooth batter forms. Bake in 8-inch rounds at 350°F for 35 minutes or until toothpick comes out clean. Let cool completely before unmolding. Cut into serving size pieces.

Assembly

Place cake slice in center of plate. Soak each layer with stewed cherry juice. Top each cake piece with cherries, and a dollop of whipped cream. Sprinkle powdered sugar to finish each plate.

KEY LIME PIE STACK

The first time we made this recipe was for a dessert cooking class. We showcased our crispy almond tuiles, and contrasted them with a creamy key lime curd and an airy whipped cream. The sweetness of the whipped cream is a must to cut the tartness of the key lime curd in this dessert. Use these tuiles to garnish any dessert, or just have them on their own.

Serves 6

Key Lime Curd

½ cup fresh key lime juice
1 tbsp finely grated fresh lime zest
1 cup sugar
1 stick unsalted butter, cut into chunks
2 tbsp cornstarch
½ tsp salt
4 large egg yolks

Place lemon juice, zest, sugar, butter, cornstarch, and salt in a mixer and blend until combined. Pour into a 2 qt saucepan over medium heat, whisking constantly. Beat egg yolks in a small bowl, then add ¼ lime mixture and continue whisking. Add yolk and lemon mixture back to saucepan, then reduce heat to low and cook, whisking constantly, until curd is thick enough to coat the back of a spoon (about 2 minutes). Transfer to a bowl, then cover surface with plastic wrap and chill.

Almond Tuiles

5 oz sugar
5 oz almonds, chopped
4 oz butter, cold
5 oz corn syrup
5 oz pastry flour

Combine dry ingredients. Combine wet ingredients. Combine the two mixtures and refrigerate batter. Roll batter into ½ inch balls, and bake on cookie sheet lined with parchment paper at 350°F until brown. Silicone baking pads also work well. Remove from sheet promptly. Store in airtight container until ready to use.

Whipped Cream

16 oz heavy cream
½ cup powdered sugar
1 tsp vanilla extract

Combine. Whip to soft peaks in a cooled bowl.

HIP ASIAN SNICKERDOODLES

My friend Judy from Rhode Island claims that her grandfather invented the Snickerdoodle. It's a great cookie, and not too hard to make. We put an Asian spin on these cookies by adding ginger.

Makes 12 cookies

Dough

½ cup butter, softened
1 cup sugar
¼ tsp baking soda
¼ tsp cream of tartar
1 egg
½ tsp vanilla extract
1½ cups all-purpose flour

Coating

4 tbsp sugar
1½ tsp cinnamon
1 tsp ground ginger

Preheat oven to 375°F. Beat butter in a mixer on medium speed for 30 seconds. Add 1 cup sugar, baking soda, and cream of tartar. Beat until combined well. Add egg and vanilla and beat until well blended. Stir in flour. Cover with plastic wrap and chill for 1 hour.

Combine the remaining 4 tbsp sugar and cinnamon with ginger. Shape the dough into 1-inch balls and roll in cinnamon sugar mixture to coat. Place balls 2 inches apart on sheet pan. Bake for 10 to 11 minutes or until edges are golden. Let cool.

Coconut Milk Tapioca Cream with Banana

The Vietnamese call this dish Che Chuoi. You can find lots of Che's in Vietnam, and they are all dessert soups flavored with various ingredients. This one is a nice flavor combination, and we make it *Hip* by caramelizing the bananas on top, adding a crunch to this basic cream dessert. You will find tapioca in many desserts all over Asia.

Serves 4

¼ cup tapioca pearls
3 cups coconut milk
2 cups heavy cream
⅓ cup sugar
4 large ripe but firm bananas
2 tbsp toasted sesame seeds
1 tbsp five-spice powder
Banana slices, for garnishing

In a bowl, soak tapioca pearls for 20 minutes in warm water. Drain.

Bring coconut milk, cream, and sugar to a boil. Add bananas and tapioca pearls and simmer, partially covered, until pearls are clear. Sprinkle five-spice powder on top of cream and stir in.

Serve warm or cold and top with sesame seeds. Place sliced bananas over cream and top with sugar. Torch or broil sugar until it is caramelized.

AUNTIE BILLIE'S APPLE PIE

In my grandfather's restaurant, one of the ladies who worked for him made the best coffee cakes and apple pies. She made them for us periodically throughout the year, even after the restaurant was gone. Although she never taught me the recipe, I tried several combinations until I came up with the one that matches hers perfectly.

Serves 8

Crust

2½ cups all-purpose flour
½ tsp salt
⅔ cup butter
6 tbsp water, cold

On a floured surface, cut in butter with flour and salt. Add water, 1 tbsp at a time until dough holds together. Divide dough in half, wrap, and place in refrigerator.

Apple Pie Filling

6 apples of your choice, cut into chunks (Granny Smiths work well)
3 tbsp butter
½ cup sugar
1 tsp cinnamon
1 tbsp corn starch
1 tbsp lemon juice

Combine all ingredients.

Assembly

Roll out two dough balls to ⅛ inch thick circles. In a deep-dish pie pan, layer bottom crust. Place apple pie filling in center of pan, and cover with top crust. Pinch edges to your choice of design. Cut slits in top of crust to allow steam to vent. Brush a beaten egg on top of crust and sprinkle sugar on top of crust before baking. Bake at 375°F for 50 to 60 minutes.

Let cool completely and serve with ice cream.

GREEN TEA CRÈME BRULEE

Our most popular exotic dessert is our tea crème brulee. We change the flavor of the tea often, but the basic recipe is the same. Once you try this recipe, you will never want plain vanilla crème brulee ever again. You can use this recipe for any flavored tea that might come to mind. Earl Grey, Thai Tea, and Black Tea all make great brulees.

Serves 12

1 qt heavy cream
9 egg yolks
1 egg
1½ cups sugar
2 tbsp green tea leaves

Combine egg yolks, ¾ cup sugar, and whole egg in a large bowl. In a heavy saucepan, heat cream, tea leaves, and remaining sugar until the mixture begins to boil. Temper egg mixture by adding a small amount of boiled cream while stirring. Add remaining cream to egg mixture, and strain. Fill ramekins* ⅔ full. Bake at 325°F in a water bath until custard sets, about 1 hour, or until brulee jiggles without running.

Refrigerate for at least 3 hours until firm. Spoon 1 tbsp of sugar evenly on each brulee. Torch each brulee until sugar caramelizes.

*Note: Ramekins are little porcelain crocks that hold oven-baked desserts. You can find them in various sizes at kitchenware stores.

ASIAN SANGRIA GRANITA

Who doesn't like a frozen dessert in the middle of a hot day? This dessert is great for a hot afternoon on the patio. If you like sangria, here is a great way to make it even better. Start this recipe on a Friday, and enjoy the end result on a Sunday afternoon.

Serves 8

1 bottle dry red wine
2 cups sake
2 cups orange juice
1 cup sugar
¼ cup brandy
½ cup triple sec or other orange liquor
1 cup apple juice or pureed fruit
Fresh diced fruit for garnish

Bring orange juice and sugar to a boil. Let cool.

Combine and freeze all ingredients over night. Scrape solid block with fork. Serve in ramekins or small bowls and garnish with fruit.

Red Tres Litchis Cake

The traditional Tres Leches is a Latin cake that is made from three milk ingredients: heavy cream, condensed milk and evaporated milk. Our version features three types of litchi ingredients. A litchi is a Southeast Asian fruit that is sweet, and has a pear-like flavor. The presentation is up to you because all the components of this dessert will work well together.

Serves 8

Cake

9 oz sugar
9 whole eggs
6 oz cake flour
3 oz corn starch
2 oz butter, melted
½ oz red food coloring

Sift dry ingredients. Whip eggs on high speed for 10 minutes. It will increase 3 times in volume. Fold in the dry ingredients. Drizzle in butter and food coloring. Place batter in cake pans of your choice. Bake at 375°F until firm to the touch, about 30 minutes for 8-inch round pans. Pour the sugared tea cream over the cake and refrigerate.

Sugared Tea Cream

2 tbsp litchi tea leaves
1 cup heavy cream
1 cup sweetened condensed milk
¼ cup sugar

Bring ingredients to a boil. Refrigerate and set aside until needed.

Tea Whipped Cream

16 oz heavy cream
2 tbsp litchi tea leaves
½ cup sugar

Sprinkle sugar over cream in a tall pot. Bring to a boil and add tea. Steep for 3 minutes, strain, and cool in refrigerator. Whip to soft peaks in a cooled bowl.

Raspberry Litchi Syrup

2 cans litchis
1 pt raspberries

Strain litchi liquid into saucepan. Reserve fruit. Add raspberries and reduce syrup by half.

Cardamom Scented Litchis

2 cans litchis
Finely ground cardamom

Dice litchis, and sprinkle cardamom over fruit. Plate components as you wish.

GUAVA BANANA SPLIT

We don't make these too often, but they are a lot of fun. Our version of a banana split has caramelized sugar on the bananas for a nice crunch. The one that you see here is made with jackfruit, or durian-flavored ice cream. Here's a basic recipe, but for the photo, we were lucky enough to find a few little longans fresh and in season.

Serves 2

1 banana
Vanilla ice cream
Chocolate ganache*
Pineapple preserves
Guava preserves
Fresh whipped cream
Maraschino cherries

Split bananas lengthwise. Caramelize with sugar. Assemble according to personal tastes.

Whipped Cream

16 oz heavy cream
½ cup powdered sugar

Combine. Whip to soft peaks in a cooled bowl.

Guava Syrup

8 oz guava paste
½ cup sugar
1 cup water

Bring ingredients to a boil. Stir, and cool for plating.

*Note: Ganache is a chocolate and milk mixture. It can be very thin, like a chocolate sauce, or very thick, like a fudge. The ratio we use here is ½ cup chocolate to 2 cups milk.

COCONUT BREAD PUDDING

We make two versions of bread pudding at the restaurant. One is savory, and one is sweet. Often, we will serve miniature versions of both when we cater events and cocktail parties. Both versions are comforting because they are hearty and warm. Here is our recipe for sweet bread pudding. To make the savory version, substitute the vanilla, cinnamon, raisins, and coconut for 2 tablespoons of rosemary or oregano. Cut the sugar to 2 cups instead of 4.

Makes 18 individual bread puddings

4 cups sugar
Water, for caramelizing
1 cup heavy cream, heated
4 eggs
1 lb Cuban or French Bread, broken into chunks
1 tsp vanilla extract
1 tsp ground cinnamon
4 oz butter, melted
6 cups milk
Pinch salt
2 tbsp brandy
1 cup shredded coconut, unsweetened
1 cup raisins, soaked in 1 cup wine
½ cup sliced or slivered almonds

Caramel Sauce

Pour 1½ cups of the sugar in saucepan with water to wet. Heat until caramelized. Add 1 cup warm cream. Stir to combine. Remove from heat.

Break up bread into chunks. Combine remaining ingredients, and add bread. Mix well. Form in ramekins and drizzle caramel sauce on top. Bake for 45 minutes. Let cool, then unmold. Serve with additional Caramel Sauce and Cream Cheese Sauce.

Cream Cheese Sauce

8 oz cream cheese
½ cup sugar
1 cup heavy cream

Heat cream cheese and whisk in sugar and cream. Serve as a sauce with bread pudding.

CURRIED SUSHI RICE PUDDING

I like the texture of sushi rice for my rice puddings. This one uses an unusual spice, curry powder, to liven up your taste buds. The light fragrance of the curry powder can be too much if you are not careful, so stick to the recipe on this one.

Serves 8

3½ qts milk
1 lb sugar
4 thin slices ginger
1 tbsp curry powder
8 oz sushi rice
1 oz corn starch
5 eggs
Pinch of salt
Sugar for brulee

Cook rice in 3 quarts of milk with curry powder, ginger, salt, and sugar until soft, approx. 20 minutes.

Combine corn starch and eggs. Heat remaining milk to boil, then temper into eggs. Combine with rice mixture and boil for one minute.

Serve in ramekins or glasses. Sprinkle sugar on top evenly, and use torch to brulee for a great presentation.

Coconut Puree

½ cup coconut, grated and unsweetened (lightly toasted)
½ cup sugar
¼ cup water

Bring ingredients to a boil. Puree and serve with rice pudding.

HONEY TOFFEE APPLE CAKE

Every classic Chinese restaurant has a version of toffee apples, usually fried and dipped in toffee. Here's our version in a sliceable cake, topped with some fresh whipped cream. Try serving the cake warm with your favorite ice cream.

Makes one 8-inch cake

1¾ cups all-purpose flour
1 tsp cinnamon
1½ tbsp baking powder
½ cup +2 tbsp soft butter
1 cup sugar
⅓ cup honey
2 eggs
1 tsp vanilla extract
2 lbs apples, sliced
½ cup toffee chips
Juice of 1 lemon

Grease one 8-inch cake pan and line bottom with parchment.

Sift flour, cinnamon, and baking powder together. Cream together butter and sugar. Add eggs, one at a time. Add vanilla, honey, and flour gradually.

Toss apples with lemon juice and cinnamon.

Layer apples and mix in pan. Sprinkle toffee chips throughout. Spread evenly. Bake at 350°F for 50 minutes. Let cool for 20 minutes on a wire rack. Slice and serve.

Whipped Topping

2 cups heavy whipping cream
½ cup powdered sugar
1 tsp vanilla extract

Use a very cold bowl and a very cold whisk, and whip to soft peaks.

Carrot Cake

One of my favorite cakes is carrot cake and it is a fabulous ending to any meal. In college, my housemate and I would treat ourselves to a carrot cake from our local bakery on special occasions. Once I learned how to make this recipe, there was no turning back. Carrot cake does have a lot of ingredients, but it's pretty easy to make, and the result is delicious.

Makes one 3 layer cake, serves 8

Cake

2 cups all-purpose flour
2 tsp baking soda
1¼ tsp salt
2 tsp ground cinnamon
4 eggs
2 cups sugar
1 cup oil
2 cups shredded carrots
2 cups crushed pineapple
1 cup shredded coconut

Cream Cheese Frosting

1 lb unsalted butter
1 lb cream cheese
½ lb powdered sugar
1 tsp vanilla extract

Cream butter and sugar together. Add cream cheese, one ounce at a time, while mixer is still on. Add vanilla extract and combine well.

Three 9-inch cake pans, lined with parchment.

Preheat oven to 350°F. Combine flour, baking soda, salt, and cinnamon.

In a separate bowl, beat eggs and sugar together. Add oil and stir together. Stir in the dry ingredients gradually. Add carrots, pineapple, and coconut. Divide the mixture into 3 pans.

Bake for 25 minutes or until toothpick inserted in the center comes out clean.

Assembly

Cut cake layers in half horizontally and frost.

THE REAL CHINESE ALMOND COOKIES

My grandfather made Almond Cookies in his restaurants from scratch. Although he was not a baker and had no formal baking training, his cookies always turned out delicious. Unfortunately, I never learned his recipe. However, through a few trials and errors, I came up with this recipe, which closely resembles his. You'll find yourself eating more than one. The classic Chinese way of making these cookies is with lard. You may substitute shortening or butter, if you wish.

Makes 2 dozen cookies

2 cups all-purpose flour
1 tsp baking powder
½ tsp baking soda
½ lb shortening or lard
¾ cup sugar
½ cup brown sugar
1 egg
1 tsp almond extract
½tsp vanilla extract
Blanched almonds
Egg yolk for brushing

Using a stand mixer, cream sugars and shortening until fluffy. Add extracts and egg. Slowly add sifted flour, baking soda and baking powder to form a soft dough. Roll into a log, cover and refrigerate.

Cut dough into 1-inch pieces, and roll into balls. Place balls about 2 inches apart on parchment-lined cookie sheet.

Press an almond into each ball, if desired. Brush with egg yolk.

Bake at 350°F oven until golden.

BLUE BAMBOO INDEX